SAMUEL BECKETT

Waiting for Godot

LAWRENCE GRAVER

Professor of English, Williams College

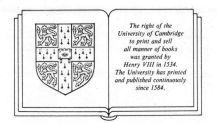

The right of the
University of Cambridge
to print and sell
all manner of books
was granted by
Henry VIII in 1534.
The University has printed
and published continuously
since 1584.

CAMBRIDGE UNIVERSITY PRESS

Cambridge
New York   New Rochelle   Melbourne   Sydney

Published by the Press Syndicate of the University of Cambridge
The Pitt Building, Trumpington Street, Cambridge CB2 1RP
32 East 57th Street, New York, NY 10022, USA
10 Stamford Road, Oakleigh, Melbourne 3166, Australia

© Cambridge University Press 1989

First published 1989

Printed in Great Britain at the University Press, Cambridge

British Library cataloguing in publication data
Graver, Lawrence
Samuel Beckett, Waiting for Godot. −
(Landmarks of world literature).
1. Drama in French. Beckett, Samuel, 1906– .
En attendant Godot.
I. Title   II. Series
842′.914

Library of Congress cataloguing in publication data
Graver, Lawrence, 1931–
Samuel Beckett, Waiting for Godot / Lawrence Graver.
      p.   cm. − (Landmarks of world literature)
Bibliography.
ISBN 0–521–35513–3. − ISBN 0–521–35775–6 (pbk.)
1. Beckett, Samuel, 1906– En attendant Godot. I. Title.
II. Series.
PQ2603.E378E645   1989
842′.914 − dc 19   88–37130   CIP

ISBN 0 521 35513 3 hard covers
ISBN 0 521 35775 6 paperback

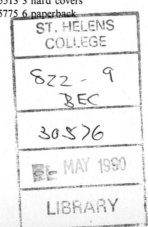

GG

For Suzanne

Contents

Preface

Anyone who writes about *Waiting for Godot* becomes a participant in an international critical colloquium that has been in session uninterruptedly since 1953. My specific debts are noted in the text and bibliography, but I want here to acknowledge how much my own thinking about the play has been continually shaped by the work of Ruby Cohn, Colin Duckworth, John Fletcher, Martin Esslin, Hugh Kenner, and James Knowlson.

To four readers of this essay, I owe very special thanks: my wife and colleague, Suzanne, who has always been my most devoted and discriminating critic; my daughter, Elizabeth, whose keen intelligence and fine French improved the text at many points; my friend and colleague, John Reichert, who makes better sense of literature than most people; and Peter Stern, friend and editor, who encouraged this study and gave it a wonderfully attentive and helpful early reading.

For readers in England and the United States, I have provided page citations for both the Faber and Faber edition, published in London, and the Grove Press edition, published in New York (indicated in the text as F and G).

Chronology

	Beckett's life and work	*Historical and cultural events*
1906	Samuel Barclay Beckett born at Foxrock, near Dublin, on April 13 (Good Friday), the second son of William Frank Beckett, a quantity surveyor, and Mary, neé Roe, a former nurse. The family is middle-class Protestant and well-off.	Death of Henrik Ibsen. First performances of G. B. Shaw's *Caesar and Cleopatra* and *The Doctor's Dilemma*; of W. B. Yeats' *Deirdre* and of Frank Wedekind's *Spring's Awakening*. Liberal government, Campbell-Bannerman Prime Minister.
1907		J. M. Synge, *Playboy of the Western World.* Yeats, *The Unicorn from the Stars.* August Strindberg writes *The Ghost Sonata.*
1909		Death of Synge.
1910		B. Russell and A. N. Whitehead, *Principia Mathematica.* Igor Stravinsky, *The Firebird.*
1913		Marcel Proust, *Swann's Way.* D. H. Lawrence, *Sons and Lovers.* Stravinsky, *Rite of Spring.*
1914		Outbreak of World War I.

1916	Earlsfort House School, Dublin.	Easter Uprising in Ireland. James Joyce, *Portrait of the Artist as a Young Man*. First performance of Yeats, *At the Hawks Well*.
1917		Revolution in Russia. U.S.A. enters the war. Balfour Declaration on Palestine. T. S. Eliot, *Prufrock and Other Observations*. Yeats, *The Wild Swans at Coole*.
1918		Armistice — World War I.
1920	Portora Royal School.	Civil war in Ireland.
1921		Irish Free State established. Luigi Pirandello, *Six Characters in Search of an Author*.
1922		Death of Proust. T. S. Eliot, *The Waste Land*. Joyce, *Ulysses*. Yeats, *Later Poems* and *The Player Queen*.
1923–7	Studies modern languages at Trinity College, Dublin. Active in Modern Language Society; plays cricket and golf; wins prizes at graduation.	Nobel Prize to Yeats. Sean O'Casey, *Juno and the Paycock*. Shaw, *Saint Joan*. Death of Franz Kafka (1924). Kafka, *The Trial* (posthumous). O'Casey, *The Plough and the*

		Stars (1926). Antonin Artaud and Roger Vitrac found the *Théâtre Alfred Jarry* in Paris. Lindbergh flies Atlantic.
1928	Teaches for two terms at Campbell College, Belfast. Goes to Paris to take up exchange lectureship at *l'Ecole normale supérieure*. Meets James Joyce and writers associated with *transition* magazine.	Bertolt Brecht, *Threepenny Opera*. O'Casey, *The Silver Tassie*. Jean Giraudoux, *Amphitryon 38*. Death of Adolphe Appia. Death of Thomas Hardy. Lawrence, *Lady Chatterley's Lover*. Aldous Huxley, *Point Counter Point*. Yeats, *The Tower*.
1929	Publishes essay 'Dante . . . Bruno. Vico . . Joyce'.	World-wide depression. T. S. Eliot, 'Dante'. Yeats, *A Packet for Ezra Pound*.
1930	Wins £10 prize from Hours Press for 'Whoroscope' a poem spoken by René Descartes. Returns to Dublin to become Assistant in French at Trinity College.	T. S. Eliot, *Ash Wednesday*. William Empson, *Seven Types of Ambiguity*. Auden, *Poems*. Harold Pinter born. Brecht writes *Fall of the City of Mahagonny*. D. H. Lawrence dies.
1931	His first dramatic work, *Le Kid*, a parody of Corneille, (written with Georges Pelorson) is performed in Dublin.	Yeats, *The Dreaming of the Bones* and *The Cat and the Moon*. Virginia Woolf, *The Waves*. André Obey, *Noah*. Death of Arnold Bennett.
1932	Begins first novel, *Dream of Fair to Middling Women* (unfinished).	Roosevelt president of the U.S.A. T. S. Eliot, *Selected Essays*. Artaud manifestos. Death of Lady Gregory.

Year		
1933	Death of William Beckett, who leaves his son an annual annuity of £200.	Hitler becomes chancellor of Germany. T. S. Eliot, *Sweeney Agonistes*. Federico García Lorca, *Blood Wedding*.
1934	*More Pricks Than Kicks*, stories, published in London.	T. S. Eliot, *The Rock*. Nobel Prize to Pirandello. Lorca, *Yerma*.
1935	*Echo's Bones and Other Precipitates*, poems, published in Paris.	T. S. Eliot, *Murder in the Cathedral*.
1936		Spanish civil war begins. Nobel Prize to Eugene O'Neill.
1937	Begins a play, *Human Wishes*, about the relationship of Dr Johnson and Mrs Thrale, but abandons it after one scene. Stabbed by a pimp on a Paris street. Visited in hospital by Suzanne Deschevaux-Dumesnil who later becomes his wife.	Chamberlain prime minister. Destruction of Guernica. David Jones, *In Parenthesis*. George Orwell, *The Road to Wigan Pier*. Giraudoux, *Electra*. Tom Stoppard (Thomas Sträussler) born.
1938	*Murphy*, his first completed novel, is published in London after many rejections.	Munich agreement. Jean-Paul Sartre, *La Nausée*. Yeats, *Purgatory*. Artaud, *The Theatre and its Double*.
1939–45	Beckett active in French resistance group gathering information about German troop movements. When group is threatened by	Germany invades Poland. World War II begins. Death of Yeats.

	Gestapo, he and Suzanne flee to the South, where they live until the end of the war. During this period, he writes *Watt* in English and a set of poems in French.	Paris occupied. Battle of Britain. Death of Aurélien Lugné-Poë. Death of Joyce (1941). Brecht, *Mother Courage*. Germany invades Russia. America enters the war. Albert Camus, *The Myth of Sisyphus* (1942). First atomic bomb exploded over Hiroshima. End of World War II.
1946	Back in Paris. Begins writing regularly in French. In what he was later to call 'the siege in the room', he writes three short stories, two short novels; a play, *Eleuthéria*; and the works that will make him famous: *Molloy*, *Malone meurt*, *En attendant Godot*, and *L'Innommable*.	Renaud-Barrault company founded. Death of Gerhart Hauptmann. Sartre, *Men Without Shadows*. O'Neill, *The Iceman Cometh*. Genet, *The Maids* (1947). State of Israel proclaimed. Death of Artaud (1948). Czechoslovakia communist. Brecht founds *Berliner* Ensemble. Ionesco, *The Bald Soprano*. Death of Shaw (1950).
1951	*Molloy* and *Malone meurt* published.	Ionesco, *The Lesson*.
1952	*En attendant Godot* published in Paris.	Ionesco, *The Chairs*. Coronation of Elizabeth II.
1953	January 5 – the world première in Paris of *En attendant Godot*, directed by Roger Blin. *Warten auf Godot* tours Germany. *L'Innommable* and *Watt* published.	Death of Stalin. Korean War ends. T. S. Eliot, *The Confidential Clerk*. Arthur Adamov, *Professor Taranne*. Death of Eugene O'Neill. Ionesco, *Victims of Duty*.

1954	*Waiting for Godot* in Beckett's translation is published in New York.	Algerian civil war (to 1962). Berliner Ensemble plays in Paris. Ionesco, *Amédée*. Nobel Prize to Hemingway.
1955	First English production of *Waiting for Godot*, Arts Theatre Club, in London, directed by Peter Hall. *Molloy* published in English in New York.	Federal Republic of West Germany becomes sovereign state. Death of Paul Claudel. Adamov, *Ping-pong*.
1956	First American production of *Waiting for Godot* directed by Alan Schneider, at the Coconut Grove Playhouse, Miami.	Hungarian uprising. Suez Canal crisis. Death of Brecht. Osborne, *Look Back in Anger*. O'Neill, *Long Day's Journey Into Night*.
1957	The radio play, *All That Fall*, broadcast on the BBC. World premiere of *Fin de Partie* in French at the Royal Court Theatre, London.	Creation of Common Market. First Russian space flight. Jean Genet, *The Blacks*. Osborne, *The Entertainer*. N. F. Simpson, *A Resounding Tinkle*. Nobel Prize to Camus.
1958	First English production of *Endgame* in New York. Première of *Krapp's Last Tape* in London.	Pinter, *The Birthday Party*. Berlin airlift. De Gaulle president of France. Nobel Prize to Boris Pasternak.
1959	*Embers* broadcast on the BBC.	John Arden, *Serjeant Musgrave's Dance*.

Year		
1961	*Comment c'est*. *Poems in English*. Première of *Happy Days* in New York.	National Theatre Company founded, housed at Old Vic.
1962	*Words and Music* broadcast on BBC. British première of *Happy Days*.	Edward Albee, *Who's Afraid of Virginia Woolf?* Ionesco, *Exit the King*. Martin Esslin's *Theatre of the Absurd*, Ionesco, *Notes and Counternotes*.
1963	Première of *Play* in German (*Spiel*).	Assassination of Kennedy.
1964	*Film*, directed by Alan Schneider and starring Buster Keaton, is produced in New York.	Death of O'Casey. Polish Lab Theatre founded by Grotowski. Peter Weiss, *Marat/Sade*.
1965	*Come and Go*.	Pinter, *The Homecoming*.
1966	Directs first production of his work *Va et vient* (*Come and Go*) in Paris.	Peter Handke, *Insulting the Audience*. Deaths of Gordon Craig and André Breton.
1967	*No's Knife*. Directs *Endgame* at Schiller Theater, Berlin.	Stoppard, *Rosencrantz and Guildenstern are Dead*.
1968	*Watt* in French published in Paris.	Student protests in Paris. Peter Brook, *The Empty Space*.
1969	Awarded Nobel Prize for Literature.	
1970	Directs *Krapp's Last Tape* in Paris and *Happy Days* in Berlin.	U.S.A. lands men on the moon. Joe Orton, *What the Butler Saw*. Death of De Gaulle. David Storey, *Home*. Pinter, *Old Times* (1971).

1972	Première of *Not I* at Lincoln Center, New York. *The Lost Ones*.	U.S.A. troops leave Vietnam. Stoppard, *Jumpers*.
1974	*Mercier and Camier*.	Stoppard, *Travesties*.
1975	Directs *Warten auf Godot* at Schiller Theater, Berlin.	Death of Thornton Wilder. Pinter, *No Man's Land*. David Mamet, *American Buffalo*.
1976	*That Time* and *Footfalls* (directed by himself) open in London.	National Theatre opens on the South Bank in London. Deaths of André Malraux and Raymond Queneau.
1977	*Ghost Trio* and . . . *but the clouds* . . . broadcast on BBC TV.	
1978		Pinter, *Betrayal*.
1979	Directs *Happy Days* with Billie Whitelaw in London.	Soviets invade Afghanistan.
1980	*A Piece of Monologue* plays in New York. *Company*.	Iraq invades Iran. Death of Sartre. Pinter, *The Hothouse*.
1981	*Mal Vu Mal Dit (Ill Seen Ill Said)*. Première of *Rockaby* in Buffalo, New York and *Ohio Impromptu* in Columbus, Ohio. Directs *Quad* on German television.	Mitterand elected president of France. Sadat assassinated; Mubarak president of Egypt. Nobel Prize to Elias Canetti.

1982	Première of *Catastrophe* at Avignon Festival.
	Israel invades Lebanon. Falkland Island war.
1983	*Worstward Ho. Nacht und Träume.* Première of *What Where* in New York.
	Thatcher begins second term as prime minister. Nobel prize to William Golding. Death of Tennessee Williams.
1984	*Collected Shorter Plays.* Supervises San Quentin Drama Workshop production of *Waiting for Godot* in London.
	Indira Gandhi assassinated. Reagan re-elected. Death of Roger Blin. Britain approves Ulster pact.
1985	Gorbachev General Secretary of Communist Party in Soviet Union.
1986	Plays by Beckett performed at festivals and conferences around the world to celebrate his 80th birthday.
	Space shuttle *Challenger* explodes in U.S.A. Pinter, *One for the Road*. Death of Alan Schneider. Peter Brook's production of the *Mahabharata* at Avignon festival.
1987	*Waiting for Godot*, directed by Michael Rudman and starring Alec McCowen and John Alderton plays at National Theatre, London.
	Thatcher begins third term as prime minister. Treaty on intermediate-range weapons signed by the United States and the Soviet Union.
1988	*L'Image* published in Paris. *Waiting for Godot*, directed by Mike Nichols and starring Steve Martin, Robin Williams, F. Murray Abraham and Bill Irwin, plays at Lincoln Center in New York.
	Reagan and Gorbachev summit meeting in Moscow. Soviet troop withdrawal from Afghanistan. Cease-fire in war between Iran and Iraq. Pinter, *Mountain Language*.

Chapter 1

En attendant Godot/Waiting for Godot: genesis and reception

On the night of 5 January 1953, a small but eager audience gathered at the tiny Théâtre de Babylone on the Boulevard Raspail to see a new play by a forty-six-year-old, widely published but little known Irish expatriate then living in Paris and writing in French. A year and a half earlier, Samuel Beckett had created a stir among critics with the powerful, mysteriously evocative novels, *Molloy* and *Malone meurt*; the previous February, scenes from the new play, *En attendant Godot*, had been broadcast on the radio, and a full text appeared in October. Yet despite the anticipation and enthusiasm (and the fact that thirty reviewers were at the dress rehearsal the day before), no one in the audience on that winter night (least of all the author himself) could have thought that this, Beckett's first staged play, would within a few years be performed in hundreds of theatres all over the world and become one of the most widely discussed, influential literary landmarks of the twentieth century.

The story of the genesis and reception of *En attendant Godot* — of its place in Beckett's development as a writer and its impact on the contemporary theatre — is fascinating yet not easy to relate. The play comes in the middle of the career of a major writer who for half a century has moved in a sinuous way through countries, languages and genres (distinguishing himself in all of them), and its extraordinary influence on the way people look at and think about drama is still being felt.

Beckett at the beginning

Samuel Barclay Beckett was born on Good Friday, 13 April 1906, at Foxrock near Dublin. His parents came from well-to-do Protestant families and the boy was educated at the prestigious Portora Royal School in Enniskillin. Between 1923 and 1927, he studied modern languages at Trinity College, Dublin, won several prizes and was appointed to an exchange lectureship at *l'Ecole normale supérieure* in Paris. In France Beckett soon became friends with his older countryman, James Joyce, already famous for *Ulysses* and now writing *Finnegans Wake*, and got to know some of the literary people associated with the avant-garde magazine *transition*.

When Beckett began publishing in the late 1920s and early 1930s, he must have looked very much like dozens of other young writers apprenticed to the high modernist avant-garde. He had studied French and Italian at Trinity College, picked up German on his travels, read some philosophy and aesthetics, knew Dante and the symbolist poets, and valued the work of Proust, Joyce and T. S. Eliot above that of all other contemporary authors. At first glance, the poems, essays and stories he wrote before 1935 seem to share many of the assumptions of the literature he so warmly admired. Knotty, multi-lingual, suspicious of traditional realism, ironical and teasingly obscure, they flaunt elusiveness like a hard-won badge of honour; and what so often makes them difficult to grasp is their persistent, extravagant bookishness. The sardonic university wit − his head jammed with quotations and paradoxes − appears hardly able to write a sentence without relating his thoughts and feelings to the ideas and language of other literary men and women.

His first essay, 'Dante . . . Bruno . Vico . . Joyce' (1929), is an audacious, sometimes brilliant, often opaque contribution to a symposium promoting *Finnegans Wake* ('Our Exagmination Round His Factification for Incamination of Work in Progress'). His prize-winning poem, 'Whoroscope' (1930), a monologue spoken by René Descartes, subverts serious thoughts about time and cognition with the jaunty suggestion that philosophy may be promiscuous play; but the game comes (like 'The Waste Land') with twenty less than forthcoming footnotes needed for the playing. The short critical book, *Proust* (1931), is brilliantly aphoristic yet heavily abstract; written, Beckett said acidly years later, 'in a cheap flashy philosophic jargon'. And his volume of short stories, *More Pricks Than Kicks* (1934) — though freshly inventive by paragraph or page — finally sinks under its own persistent displays of polyglot erudition. As Beckett summed it up two decades later: his literary output in the early 1930s was 'the work of a young man with nothing to say and an itch to make'.

Admittedly, much of young Beckett's unbridled bookishness reflects genuine learning and is designed to satirize intellectual pretensions. Nonetheless, the dominant effect of the literary high jinks is stifling. Allusions — random or relevant, esoteric or familiar — come tumbling along so quickly, exist so often only for their own ingenuity, that the elements necessary to sustain a story or a poem (narrative line, the progression of an image, the growth of a character or an emotion, deepening reflections) rarely take shape. It is no surprise that many early reviewers saw Beckett's extravagant cleverness and sophistication as the major obstacle to his finding his own voice as a writer. When these books of the early 1930s are read now, it is usually because they are by the man who later wrote *Molloy, Malone Dies, The Unnamable, Waiting for Godot, Endgame* and the matchless fiction and drama that came after.

The surprise, though, is that no one knew this better than young Beckett himself. At the same time that the early books lavishly demonstrate his wide reading and his debt to the inclusive, style-conscious work of his modernist masters, they also reveal a powerful uneasiness about the verbal strategies to which he seems so passionately devoted. Because of the affectation and surface glitter, Beckett's argument with himself can go unnoticed, but it is there and gradually emerges as one of the most dramatic and fruitful subjects of his later writing.

His scepticism was based on two related perceptions: that his tendency towards intellectual self-display was an elaborate form of evasion, a screen to keep him from dealing with emotions at the heart of his experience of contemporary life; and that many of the assumptions inherent in the modernist works he admired ran counter to his own evolving ideas of what a literature reflecting that life should be. In Beckett's view, Joyce and Proust were encyclopaedists, who — writing about fragmentation and loss — wished to get everything into their novels by colossal acts of imaginative recovery. Their ambitions were omnipotent, god-like; their creations second worlds, more orderly and conceivably even superior to the first. Under Joyce's masterful direction, language seemed limitless in its powers of analysis and suggestion, and vast learning was a way to see behind loss and disjunction those mysterious, submerged linkages between past and present that might possibly unify modern life.

For Beckett, though, in the 1930s, ideas about comprehensiveness, omnipotence and unity were daily becoming less applicable, more foreign. His own experience was confirming an opposite set of facts about life and how a writer should deal with it in his books. As he himself was later to express it (in prose recounted by Israel Schenker):

. . . Joyce is a superb manipulator of material — perhaps the greatest. He was making words do the absolute maximum of work. There isn't a syllable that's superfluous. The kind of work I do is one in which I'm not master of my material. The more Joyce knew the more he could. He's tending toward omniscience and omnipotence as an artist. I'm working with impotence, ignorance. I don't think impotence has been exploited in the past. There seems to be a kind of esthetic axiom that expression is achievement — must be an achievement. My little exploration is that whole zone of being that has always been set aside by artists as something unusable — as something by definition incompatible with art.

(Graver and Federman, p. 148)

To explain in detail how Beckett eventually shed his excess literary baggage as he set out to explore a previously uncharted 'zone of being' is beyond the scope of this single study of his best-known work. But one can point out the most important stages along the way. The process started with the composition of *Murphy* (1938), a dazzling philosophical comedy on the themes of the nature of desire and of learning divided against itself. The protagonist of Beckett's finest early book is a zany anti-intellectual young intellectual who tries, by rocking bound and naked in a chair, to escape from the confusing contingency of the world into the sovereignty and freedom of his own mind. But Murphy's bizarre 'idea' of his own mind (a hollow sphere, 'windowless as a monad') and his methods of flight are themselves products of considerable reading and experience of the world. When he is farcically dispatched by an exploding gas heater, the last joke (and a learned one) is on him, for, as the narrator tells us, the word 'gas' derives from the Greek word for 'chaos', just as Murphy's own name derives from the Greek for 'form'.

Murphy's death occurs halfway through the book, and at that point the novel moves away from a dependence on the density of erudition so central to its original style and subject-matter. The two closing chapters (especially the last) are surprisingly free of the wordplay and recondite allusions so integral to all that went before. The last words of the book, 'all out', refer in context to the cry of rangers closing a park where Murphy's girl friend is walking, but they might also be read as Beckett's own farewell to his apprentice art.

Murphy was obviously a watershed book for Beckett: at once the perfection of his baroque early manner and an announcement of a new departure. But if it stands between two phases of his development as a writer, it also (in retrospect) is evidence of the difficulty Beckett had in getting beyond its achievement. After he had published *Murphy* in 1938, Beckett found writing increasingly more difficult. During the next seven years he published only a few poems and reviews and worked obsessively on a remarkable novel about linguistic disintegration called *Watt* (which did not appear until 1953).

But the most important fact about Beckett's literary life during this period is that he began to write poetry and fiction in French, and it was in his adopted language that he broke the deadlock and found his mature voice. Between January and December 1946, he completed the stories 'La Fin', 'L'Expulsé', and 'Le Calmant'; the short novels, *Mercier et Camier* and *Premier Amour*, and the play *Eleuthéria*. Immediately after that, between 1947 and 1950, he wrote *Molloy*, *Malone meurt*, *En attendant Godot*, and *L'Innommable* – the books on which much of his reputation as a major writer rests. In later years, to the often posed question 'why did you turn from English to French?' Beckett has given many different answers, but a consistent theme runs through all of them. 'It is easier', he told Nicholas Gessner in 1957, 'to write without style in French.' Three years later he explained to Herbert Blau that French appealed to him because it had 'the right weakening effect', and he also remarked to Richard Coe that he was afraid of English because 'you couldn't help writing poetry in it'. In 1962, responding more fully to the same question, Beckett told Lawrence Harvey that

for him, an Irishman, French represented a form of weakness by comparison with his mother tongue. Besides, English because of its very richness holds out the temptation to rhetoric and virtuosity, which are merely words mirroring themselves complacently, Narcissus-like. The relative asceticism of French seemed more appropriate to the expression of being, undeveloped, unsupported somewhere in the depths of the microcosm.   (Harvey, p. 196)

And in 1968, he told his friend Ludovic Janvier: 'I took up writing again – in French – with the desire of impoverishing myself still further.'

Being, undeveloped, unsupported somewhere in the depths of the microcosm – this was to be Beckett's subject for the rest of his writing life, and his distinctive signature as an artist was to be his astonishing facility for inventing resonant new images to express the paradox of the fathomless limits of the modern consciousness of being.

Paris 1946–8

The breakthrough for Beckett came when he returned to Paris at the end of World War II, having lived in seclusion at Roussillon in the Vaucluse during much of the German occupation of France. Simultaneously with his pursuit of the 'relative asceticism' of French, he also discovered a new subject-matter and a new voice. The decisive clue to what this subject-matter might be seems to have come to Beckett on a stormy night in early spring 1946, when – during a visit to Ireland – he stood on a jetty in Dublin harbour and had a startling vision that prefigured the direction of his future work.

As he was to dramatize it twelve years later in *Krapp's Last Tape*, Beckett perceived that those dark and tumultuous aspects of his own personality which he had always 'struggled to keep under' were in reality his most precious possessions. From then on, he realized, he would have to write not about the macrocosm, the world around him, but rather about the recesses of his own self: 'the within, all that inner space one never sees'. For this adventurous excavation he would be compelled to discard the all-knowing, sly, third-person literary voices of his early stories and novels and invent in fictional monologue a new voice: the solitary voice of the 'non-knower, the non-can-er'.

When Beckett returned to his Paris apartment in May 1946, he began writing quickly and with uncharacteristic *élan*. In a matter of months, fighting what he called 'the battle of the soliloquy', he fashioned in the *nouvelles* and *Molloy* the astonishing fictional voice that was to be his first great contribution to modern European literature. Through this voice he would try to speak more exactingly about inwardness than he had ever done before, and the paradox explicit in the effort would be at the heart of the enterprise. He could express himself only through a fictional other because one of his most powerful intuitions about himself was a consciousness of experiencing 'existence by proxy' – always in terms of what was not there, of something or someone absent.

Years later Beckett elaborated on these feelings and beliefs in a conversation with the critic Lawrence Harvey, whose account of the occasion is of great value. According to Harvey, Beckett repeatedly used the phrase 'existence by proxy' to express his sense of the unreality of life on the surface. Out on the street he often felt unable to take a single step without feeling that someone else was doing the walking. The sense of going through the physical motions, yet of being in some fundamental way absent, was overpowering. Beckett also connected this feeling to the arguments of the eighteenth-century idealist philosopher George Berkeley (also a Trinity College alumnus), and he suggested that perhaps it was an Irish trait to be sceptical both of the natural world as given and of the perceiving subject as well. Harvey concludes:

Along with this sense of existence by proxy goes 'an unconquerable intuition that being is so unlike what one is standing up', an intuition of 'a presence, embryonic, undeveloped, of a self that might have been but never got born, an *être manqué*'.   (Harvey, p. 247)

It was through invented surrogates (called at first Molloy, then Moran, Malone, and the Unnamable) that Beckett most memorably dramatized these feelings and ideas in fiction. In his own formulation, each figure was 'the narrator/narrated', a voice speaking as if by compulsion, as if prompted by, or in the service of, some mysterious agent outside or perhaps even inside himself. The ancient and destitute Molloy, for instance, announces on page one that he is in his mother's room (an enclosed place that mirrors the mind) trying to write an account of how he got there for some shadowy person who appears every week to pick up the pages. The epitome of disillusioned self-consciousness, he tells a story that is by turns (and often at the same time) grotesque, lyrical, wildly comic, feverish and serene; and yet he never manages to tell us what he originally had set out to relate.

Malone, even older, is confined to bed in the room of what may be a nursing home, where he tries to write down a sequence of stories to pass the time until he dies. Like Molloy, he is an inspired inventor of marvellous and frightful tales, and his narrative, too, is both progressive and self-cancelling, undermined by his corrosive suspicion of the only tool he has: his own language. Most exacerbated of all is the Unnamable, *literally* the voice of disembodied consciousness, who tries with defiant, panic-stricken single-mindedness to talk about himself without recourse to the fictional surrogates (Murphy, Watt, Molloy, Moran, Malone, etc.) who had previously stood in for him. But he discovers that the embryonic pre-sence which might be his abortive self can only be expressed in terms of stories – linguistic inventions he distrusts and tries to (but can't) forswear.

Taken together, *Molloy, Malone Dies*, and *The Unnamable* make up one of the most daring and fiercely imagined creations in modern literature. And both for the writer and the reader, one of the most exacting. Not-knowing and not-being-able has never been described before with such vigilance and pertinacity, and with such astonishing linguistic flair. But in the persistence with which this *Trilogy* expressed what Beckett once called 'the tragi-comedy of a solipsism that will not capitulate', it brought him in the late 1940s to still another artistic impasse. The further in he went, the more sceptical he seemed to become about what he found there and especially about his ability to locate a language to convey it.

Godot in Paris, London, and New York

If Beckett went into the dark to find *Molloy* and *Malone meurt*, he came (in his own phrase) 'back into the light' to discover *En attendant Godot*. He began it 'as a relaxation from the awful prose I was writing at that time', to escape from 'the wildness and rulelessness of the novels'. Unexpectedly, the play came quickly, with few revisions, between 9 October 1948 and 29 January 1949. 'I needed a habitable place', he told a friend, 'and I found it on the stage.'

But in the late winter of 1949, the particular stage on which *Godot* might appear was not easy to locate. Out of despair at the rejection of nearly everything he had written in French for the past three years, Beckett suspended efforts to interest publishers or producers in his work. However, his friend Suzanne Deschevaux-Dumesnil regularly made the rounds in his stead, taking typescripts of *Eleuthéria* and *En attendant Godot* to theatre people who might conceivably put them on. The first half-dozen producers approached turned down the plays for various reasons: *Eleuthéria* was too cumbersome, costly, and hard to follow; the bizarre *Godot* had no roles for women and no plot to speak of. Without a story line or characters with whom to identify, neither play was likely to interest enough people to make money.

After these discouragements, Deschevaux-Dumesnil proposed that they approach Roger Blin, a respected French actor and director. In 1935 Blin had appeared in Antonin Artaud's adaptation of Shelley's *The Cenci*, a much talked-about avant-garde production. He then studied mime with Jean-Louis Barrault and had just recently staged Strindberg's *The Ghost Sonata*. Artaud, Barrault, Strindberg — the names of such notable theatrical innovators led Deschevaux-Dumesnil to think that Roger Blin might be receptive enough to look at the unconventional manuscripts she was carrying about. Beckett, having suffered so many rejections, remained wary, but he did go twice to see the director's *Ghost Sonata* at the Gaîté-Montparnasse. Deschevaux-Dumesnil left the manuscripts at Blin's office and some weeks later was happily surprised by his positive response.

At first Blin thought of trying to produce *Eleuthéria* because it was the more traditional of the two plays, but since it had seventeen characters, a divided stage, elaborate props and complicated lighting, he eventually decided that it might be wiser to try to stage *Godot*. Here, he felt, 'there were only four actors and they were bums. They could wear their own clothes if it came to that, and I wouldn't need anything but a spotlight and a bare branch for a tree' (Bair, p. 403).

Nonetheless, despite Blin's support, a number of obstacles remained. Several of his associates were sceptical about backing an experimental work by a writer who had never had a play staged, and they were reluctant to pledge the money. Beckett agreed, though, that Blin should hold the manuscripts and keep pursuing the possibilities. The director had a reputation for respecting the text of any play he staged, and besides, when Beckett went to see *The Ghost Sonata*, the theatre was half-empty — a sign he considered to be auspicious for the future of his own austere and idiosyncratic work.

Two years went by before sufficient money was raised and protracted negotiations for a suitable theatre completed.

Most of the funds came from a government grant of about £1,000 for the support of first plays, which Blin supplemented with money borrowed from friends. Neither he nor Beckett were to receive payment for their work as director and writer. To help stir up interest in the production, extracts from *Godot* were broadcast on ORTF in February 1952, and in October the text itself was published by Les Editions de Minuit (the small firm that had a year earlier printed *Molloy* and *Malone meurt* to unexpectedly high praise from the critics).

Contracts were signed, the play went into rehearsals and, after several cast changes, it opened on 5 January 1953, with Pierre Latour as Estragon, Lucian Raimbourg as Vladimir, Jean Martin as Lucky, and Roger Blin himself as Pozzo. The reactions of the audience on the first night and in the following weeks set the pattern for responses that were later repeated in cities around the world. Some people were baffled, bored, irritated: the play had no plot; it seemed to maunder on repetitiously to no discernible dramatic point. Others, suspecting an intellectual put-on, complained of inflated pseudo-significance and dismissed *Godot* as a coterie piece designed to please snobs who mistook obscurity and pretence for profundity. Still other playgoers nervously speculated about its meaning and constructed allegories about the death or disappearance of God based on the provocations of Beckett's title and his specific allusions to Christianity. One bewildered reviewer, looking for a more material peg on which to hang a thesis, thought Beckett (whom he believed to be an American novelist) was portraying the miserable plight of famished tramps persecuted by farmers in the American South.

But dozens of other playgoers were exhilarated and by word of mouth or in print conveyed their enthusiasm. One of the first reviews to appear was also one of the most perceptive. Covering the play for *La Libération*, Sylvain Zegel immediately perceived the resonance of Beckett's dramatic poetry and the importance of the occasion. *En attendant Godot*, he insisted, would 'be spoken of for a long time'. A few days later, the playwright Jacques Audiberti urged everyone to see this 'perfect work which deserves a triumph', praise that was echoed by Jacques Lemarchand in *Figaro Littéraire*, when he celebrated the simplicity, humour, imaginative range and expressive power of 'this profoundly original work'.

Other reviewers were equally enthusiastic, and then, from the playwright Jean Anouilh, came the most succinct and eloquent of all the early tributes:

'Nothing happens, nobody comes, nobody goes, it's awful.' This line spoken by one of the characters in the play, provides its best summary. *Godot* is a masterpiece that will cause despair for men in general and for playwrights in particular. I think that the opening night at the Théâtre de Babylone is as important as the opening of Pirandello [*Six Characters in Search of an Author*] in Paris in 1923, presented by Pitoeff.

One can only raise one's hat − a bowler to be sure, as in the play − and pray to heaven for a little talent. The greatness, the artful playing, a style − we are 'somewhere' in the theatre. The music-hall sketch of Pascal's *Pensées* as played by the Fratellini clowns.

(Graver and Federman, p. 92)

Lively interest in *En attendant Godot* continued through the early weeks of 1953. In February, Alain Robbe-Grillet, the young novelist and theorist of the *nouveau roman*, wrote an extended essay for *Critique*, dismissing allegorical approaches to the play and insisting that Beckett's grandest achievement was his dramatization of the basic human condition: the state of 'being there'. Godot, he said, is only the person for whom the two tramps wait; and 'they will be there again the next day, and the next and the day after that . . . without future, without past, irremediably there.'

By the spring of 1953, *En attendant Godot* was 'irremediably there'. Blin took his ensemble on a successful tour of cities in Germany and Italy, with each of three light-travelling performers carrying one piece of the dismantled tree in his suitcase. Other productions were set for Germany, and after Beckett finished his translation, he signed a contract for a production in London and considered offers to have *Godot* staged in America. Suddenly at forty-six he was (like the weary protagonist of *Krapp's Last Tape*) 'getting known'.

In England, the producer Peter Glenville hoped to convince Alec Guinness and Ralph Richardson to play Vladimir and Estragon. But they were dissuaded in part by John Gielgud, who dismissed the play — in a phrase for which he later apologized — as 'a load of old rubbish', and by a memorable encounter that Richardson had with Beckett. As Richardson tells it, he had 'drawn up a sort of laundry list' of things he didn't understand, and invited Beckett to talk with him backstage at the Haymarket.

And Beckett came into my dressing room — wearing a knapsack, which was very mysterious — and I started to read through my list. You see, I like to know what I'm being asked to do. March up that hill and charge that blockhouse! Fine — but I wasn't sure which was the hill and where the blockhouse was . . . But Beckett just looked at me and said, 'I'm awfully sorry, but I can't answer any of your questions.' He wouldn't explain. Didn't lend me a hand. And then another job came up and I turned down the greatest play of my lifetime.   (*New Yorker*, 21 February 1977)

Little that happened in the spring of 1955 would have led anyone associated with the play to think they were preparing to stage a masterpiece. In addition to delays caused by actors and one producer losing interest, the production ran into trouble from the Lord Chamberlain, official censor of plays, who objected to the propriety of Beckett's language and to some physical gestures. Beckett agreed to make a few changes but resisted altering the offending dialogue between Vladimir and Estragon on the subject of erections or the essential fall of Estragon's trousers at the close. To circumvent the authority of the Lord Chamberlain, the London production opened at the private Arts Theatre Club on 3 August 1955, but some changes were made then, and again in September, when the show moved to the Criterion. On opening night, with Peter Hall directing, Vladimir was played by Paul Daneman, Estragon by Peter Woodthorpe, Lucky by Timothy Bateson, and Pozzo by Peter Bull. In his memoir, *I Know the Face, But* . . ., Bull recalled the play's reception: 'Waves of hostility came whirling over the footlights, and the mass exodus, which was to form such a feature of the run of the piece, started soon after the curtain had risen.' Relentlessly derisive, uncomprehending reviews over the next few days added to the gloom. One critic called *Godot* 'a bewildering curiosity', another saw it as one of those avant-garde works 'that tried to lift superficiality to significance through obscurity'; and a third concluded that what might be admired 'as a serious highbrow frolic' was not 'for the serious play-going public'.

On the weekend, however, Harold Hobson in the *Sunday Times* and Kenneth Tynan in *The Observer* wrote passionate appreciations that reversed the fortunes of the play and began an important new chapter in the history of its reputation. Admitting that *Godot* might strike some people as drab and undramatic, Hobson insisted that the play − in its brilliant cross-talk, haunting situation, and sad compassion − had a rare originality and beauty. 'Go and see *Waiting for Godot*', he told his readers. 'At the worst you will discover a curiosity, a four-leaved clover, a black tulip; at the best, something that will securely lodge in a corner of your mind for as long as you live.' Tynan was equally excited and eloquent. From where he sat, *Godot* marvellously 'summoned the music-hall and the parable to present a view of life which banished the sentimentality of the music-hall and the parable's fulsome uplift'; and he proudly declared himself, 'as the Spanish would say, *godotista*' (Graver and Federman, pp. 93–7).

The persuasive advocacy of Hobson and Tynan not only brought enough people to the theatre to guarantee the success of the play, but also helped begin spirited conversations about the nature and implications of Beckett's accomplishment. Playgoers argued in lobbies, wrote to the papers, and made *Godot* the talk of the town. Taking a second look, the London *Times* reviewer admitted that Beckett's 'sophisticated fantasy' appeared 'to hold last night's audience; and in the attentive silence one could almost hear the seeds of a cult growing'.

The cult, of course, was not without its scoffers. At least a third, sometimes half, of a typical audience walked out at the intermission, and the visiting American journalist, Marya Mannes, saw the play as 'typical of the self-delusion of which certain intellectuals are capable, embracing obscurity, pretense, ugliness, and negation as protective coloring for their own confusions'. The well-known playwright Terence Rattigan slyly invented an imaginary Aunt Edna, a shrewd, unpredictable representative of middle-brow theatregoers, with whom to chat about the pleasures but inflated reputation of Beckett's play.

What was the talk of the town soon became the talk of the country. On 10 February 1956, the published text was the subject of a long, anonymous article in the *Times Literary Supplement* that sparked a controversy destined to be the prototype of debates about the play that were soon to occur elsewhere. The author of the *TLS* essay (later identified as G. S. Fraser) testified to the excitement and appeal of Beckett's play, but insisted that no serious effort had yet been made to define its theme. In Fraser's view, *Waiting for Godot* is a sustained metaphor about the nature of human life and notably a metaphor 'which makes a particular appeal to the mood of liberal uncertainty which is the prevailing mood of modern Western Europe'. More concretely, however, the play is a modern morality play on permanent Christian themes. Vladimir and Estragon, in their rags, unhappiness, and persistent capacity for reflection, represent the fallen state of man and also the contemplative life. Pozzo and Lucky stand for the life of practical action erroneously adopted as an end in itself. At different moments, depending on the action of the four men, the tree stands for the Tree of Knowledge of Good and Evil, the Tree of Life, the Cross, and (when hanging is considered) the Judas Tree. The stripped, unspecified location of the action suggests that in this world no one can build an eternal city. Didi and Gogo's ambiguous attitude towards Godot – hope, fear, despair, and renewed expectation – represents the state of tension and uncertainty in which the average Christian must live in this world. Like the two thieves, Beckett's tramps must avoid both presumption and despair.

For more than a month after the appearance of the Fraser essay, the *TLS* printed letters responding to his interpretation of the play. The critic J.M.S. Tompkins agreed that *Godot* was a Christian allegory as ancient and orthodox as that of the medieval *Piers Plowman*. Each couple, she said, represents within itself the fundamental dualism of human nature and each is destined to follow the fates of the two thieves: Vladimir and Estragon will be saved because they represent the charitable; caring nature of man; Pozzo and Lucky (natural man who has made conscience his slave) are 'on the last stages of the steep slope to damnation'. Not so, said Katherine M. Wilson a week later. *Waiting for Godot* is doctrinaire existentialism, a work that presents contemporary life in its full horror so that 'the audience, finding it unendurable, may feel forced to remedy it'. According to Wilson, the existentialist philosopher Jean-Paul Sartre would call G.S. Fraser's attitude 'a typical instance of "bad faith", which attributes all our misery to God or fate – as if our human situation were given – in order to evade having to face up to our responsibility for it.' The moral of the play, she said, is framed as a question: since this is what waiting for Godot is like, must we wait for Godot?

But other correspondents would have neither the Christian nor the existentialist reading. Philip Bagby, for instance, saw Beckett 'chuckling away somewhere in France' at all these earnest attempts to extract a clear message from a play whose strength lay in its ambiguity, its refusal to offer a decisive reason to prefer either hope or despair. But even Bagby felt discomfort with his own fence-sitting argument. 'For my part,' he concluded, 'I believe that Godot does come – to those who know how to see him. But this answer I find in myself, not in the play.'

Two weeks later came a brilliant, tendentious and ultimately wrong-headed letter from William Empson, who – from his own fierce aversion to Christianity – saw *Waiting for Godot* as the expression of Beckett's disillusionment and rage at the false promises of his fierce Irish religious training. But it did not take long for other correspondents to point out that Empson's account of religious training in Ireland was hardly accurate, and besides, Beckett was a Protestant who slipped away, not a Catholic who rebelled.

The intensity that marked this exchange of letters in the *Times Literary Supplement* had also characterized the reaction of audiences when the play had opened in America a few weeks before. Although national responses to *Godot* fell into roughly similar patterns (tedium, puzzlement, vexation, delight, enthusiasm, and passionate, contentious debate), each première has its own distinctive and revealing history. Plans for an American production had begun to take shape early in 1955, when Michael Meyerberg invited Alan Schneider to direct the popular comedians Bert Lahr and Tom Ewell in a version that would open in Washington and Philadelphia and then go on to Broadway. Schneider was dubious about almost every aspect of the proposal, except the quality of the play. Meyerberg was meddlesome and mercurial; Bert Lahr was a brilliant vaudevillian with little sense of what beyond comedy Beckett's play might demand of him; and Broadway was hardly the fit destination for so unconventional a play as *Godot*.

But Schneider found the invitation too challenging to reject, and before starting rehearsals he managed to convince Beckett to meet with him in Paris to talk about his work. The encounter of writer and director began a collaboration that became one of the most fruitful in the modern theatre; over the next quarter of a century Schneider was to direct nearly all of Beckett's plays, several in their world premières. When the two men met in 1955, Beckett insisted that he could not talk in general or abstract ways about his work and would only answer concrete questions about details and textures. Asked by Schneider 'who or what is Godot', Beckett pointedly (yet insinuatingly) replied: 'If I knew, I would have said so in the play.'

Although Schneider was as well prepared as anyone could be to stage *Waiting for Godot*, the subsequent misadventures of the first American production have become legendary in contemporary theatre history. When advance sales in Washington and Philadelphia were disappointing, Meyerberg switched the opening to a new theatre in Miami, where he had been guaranteed a generous advance and where the audience would be well-heeled vacationers in search of easy diversion. Newspapers publicized the forthcoming show as 'the laugh sensation of two continents', and when Schneider tried to rehearse he found that each member of the cast had only vague or contradictory conceptions of what he was supposed to do. On opening night, 3 January 1956, the audience was, in Schneider's witty phrase, 'ambulatory', and by the beginning of the second act almost everyone was gone. For Schneider it must have been oddly consoling to hear Tennessee Williams and William Saroyan shouting 'Bravo!' in a nearly empty auditorium.

Reviews of this first performance were disdainful and the playhouse soon became known around Miami as a spot where taxi-drivers could pick up lots of early fares between the first and second acts. But gradually the handful of people who came and remained were increasingly absorbed and enthusiastic. One local hotel printed a mimeograph notice calling the play 'astonishing . . . so enormous in scope [and] so compelling as to require complete attention and in a sense devotion'.

Meyerberg's devotion to Schneider and the original cast was less steady. By the time the production reached New York in April 1956, the director and everyone else except Bert Lahr had been replaced, but nonetheless, despite rushed effort and the customary undiscerning reviews, the play created a stir. Walter Kerr of the *Herald Tribune* (29 April) breezily dismissed *Godot* as 'a cerebral tennis match' that 'can be read variously and furiously as Christian, existentialist or merely stoic allegory', and he gave most credit for the pleasures of the evening to Bert Lahr. Assuming a tone of forced liveliness, the influential *New York Times* critic, Brooks Atkinson, warned his readers not to expect him to explain 'this allegory written in a heartless modern tone . . . this mystery wrapped in an enigma' (20 April). But for all the apparent mystification, Atkinson grudgingly concluded that Beckett was 'no charlatan' and predicted that exasperated theatregoers might 'rail at the play' but they would not be able to ignore it.

Where Kerr and Atkinson suspected an allegory, Henry Hewes (in *Saturday Review*, 5 May) found one. While

Vladimir and Estragon are waiting for Godot (God), along comes a well-dressed European landowner named Pozzo (capitalist-aristocrat) followed by a wretched, exhausted slave named Lucky (labour-proletariat). 'After this pair depart, one of Godot's two sons shows up to inform Vladimir, whom he calls Mr Albert − (Schweitzer?), that Mr Godot won't come this evening but will surely come tomorrow.'

Hewes's confidence that Beckett's allegory was transparent was not shared by the hundreds of theatregoers who talked at intermission, attended symposia sponsored by the producer, urged their friends to get tickets, and avidly bought copies of the paperback recently published by Grove Press. In a few weeks, *Waiting for Godot* was being discussed less as a new play than as a cultural episode. Eric Bentley, Norman Mailer, and others wrote essays about the reception and significance of Beckett's work; and several other productions outside of New York contributed to its growing notoriety and fame.

The heat and persistence of these controversies, and of others like them elsewhere, prompted Beckett himself to make an uncharacteristically direct statement about the original reception of *Waiting for Godot* around the world. The early success of the play, he told Alec Reid in 1956, was based on a fundamental misunderstanding. Critics and public alike insisted on interpreting in allegorical or symbolic terms a play which strove at all cost to avoid definition. 'The end,' as Reid quoted Beckett, 'is to give artistic expression to something hitherto almost ignored − the irrational state of unknowingness where we exist, this mental weightlessness which is beyond reason' (*Drama Survey*, Autumn 1962).

This striking statement is entirely congruent with Beckett's aesthetic explorations in the late 1940s and 1950s, yet for all its vividness and authority, the observation does not address the question that anyone who first thinks about the early reception of *Waiting for Godot* is likely to ask. What was it about this extraordinary play that regularly provoked from audiences such vehement and diverse responses? It is with this question that the following critical analysis begins.

Chapter 2

Approaching the play

The drama of unknowingness

At evening on a country road, bare but for a low mound and a spindly tree, two men named Vladimir and Estragon – part tramp, part clown, of indeterminate age – talk fitfully about their thwarted lives and expectantly of an appointment to meet someone named Godot. While they pass the time and wait, two strangers appear, an imperious landowner called Pozzo and at the end of a rope his animal-like servant Lucky. After a bizarre, increasingly mystifying conversation (highlighted by Lucky's opaque and frenzied tirade), the master and his man move on. A boy appears to announce that Mr Godot will not come this evening but 'surely tomorrow'; and when night falls, Vladimir and Estragon contemplate suicide, decide to leave, but at the first act curtain they do not move. In Act II the basic action is similar: the next day, same time same place, Vladimir and Estragon pass the time and wait; Pozzo and Lucky – now respectively blind and dumb – again arrive and depart; the boy reappears to deliver essentially the same message (Mr Godot will not come this evening but 'surely tomorrow'); and after again considering suicide, the two men prepare to go but at the final curtain do not move.

To describe *Waiting for Godot* in this fashion is of course to say almost nothing about its originality and distinction and to ignore nearly everything of consequence about the way it makes itself felt on the stage. Yet such a summary points to something essential for an understanding of why many early theatregoers perceived the work as systematically symbolic. Stripped to its crude outline, Beckett's play certainly does sound like an allegory: a dramatic action in which events,

characters, and settings represent abstract or spiritual mean-
ings. Even for a French audience, the name Godot will be
perceived to have God in it; and the cyclical plot − on successive days two men wait for and are denied an encounter
with a shadowy figure of authority − is very close to fable.
A two-act structure so assuredly symmetrical, pairs of complementary characters in no particular place at no particular
time − how can one resist wanting to interpret this narrative
in terms of 'something else'?

Then, too, the dialogue has several conspicuous allusions
to events in the life of Christ as recounted in the New Testa-
ment. Six or seven minutes into the play, Vladimir asks
Estragon if he has ever read the Bible, particularly the
accounts in the Gospels of the two thieves, and when his
friend says no, he proceeds to lecture him on the mysteries of
salvation and damnation as they are exemplified in the most
resonant of all such stories. Later on, Estragon compares
himself to Christ; and when Vladimir observes, 'We are not
saints, but we have kept our appointment. How many people
can boast as much?', some listeners are likely to note an
allusion to the parable of the Wise and the Foolish Virgins
(Matthew 24, 25). Throughout the play there is much talk
about prayers and supplications, of goats and sheep, of the
beauty of the way and the goodness of the wayfarer, and of
a personal God with a long white beard.

The title, the sense of universal present time, the shape of
the plot and of the characters, the often pointed and tantalizing allusions − these obviously invite allegorical interpretation, and for many playgoers and readers the invitation has
proved irresistible. It is also important to remember that
when *Waiting for Godot* was first performed in the 1950s,
arguments about systems of meaning were often influenced
by a large body of philosophical and fictional writing generally
known as existentialist, which seemed at first glance to have
marked similarities to Beckett's work. Although not a cohesive
school, the existentialist writers were preoccupied with
many of the same vital issues, most notably the problem of
discovering belief in the face of radical twentieth-century

perceptions of the meaninglessness or absurdity of human life.

A characteristic existentialist response was to accept nothingness, absence, and absurdity as givens and then to explore the way human beings might self-consciously form their essence in the course of the lives they choose to lead. The origin of the inclination for transcendence was little agreed upon by such writers as Martin Heidegger, Jean-Paul Sartre, Albert Camus, and Karl Jaspers; but as Richard Shepard has described it, 'a radically negative experience is seen to contain the embryo of a positive development – though the psychological and philosophical content of that development is extremely diverse' (Fowler, p. 82).

The pervasiveness of existentialist thinking in the 1940s and 1950s was so great that any work about an individual's quest for purpose and order in life, especially in relation to an absent or a present divinity, was likely to be discussed in the context of current controversies about existence, essence, personal freedom, responsibility, and commitment. Many philosophers who were not existentialists were also absorbed by these same questions. For instance, Simone Weil, who coincidentally had been a student at *l'Ecole normale supériere* when Beckett lectured there, published a widely-read book, *Attente de Dieu* (*Waiting for God*), just at the time that Beckett and Roger Blin were trying to stage *En attendant Godot*. Yet there seems to have been no direct connection with or influence of either writer on the other. The issues were in the air.

To the ongoing existentialist arguments about meaning and belief in a profoundly sceptical time, Beckett's enigmatic yet reverberating play seemed in the mid-1950s to be making a notable contribution. So it is hardly surprising that many people tried to define concretely what they thought the playwright was saying about some of the major subjects of the debate. Yet, comprehensible as the impulse was to interpret *Waiting for Godot* allegorically, it now is clear that theatregoers were too persistently trying to link the particular provocations of the play to some specific system or structure

of thought existing outside the work itself, as if such systems
or structures would explain what this strange work was fundamentally 'about'.

Beyond question, the teasing title, the fable-like action and
the religious allusions are essential for an understanding of
the play, but not finally in the way some avid interpreters had
originally conceived. As Beckett once told Colin Duckworth,
'Christianity is a mythology with which I am perfectly
familiar, so I naturally use it' (*En attendant Godot*, p. lvii);
and to another interviewer, he remarked: 'I'm not interested
in any system. I can't see any trace of any system anywhere.'
Waiting for Godot resists not only systems but abstract ideas
as well. 'If I could have expressed the subject of [my work]
in philosophical terms,' Beckett once said, 'I wouldn't have
had any reason to write [it]' (Graver and Federman, pp. 217,
219).

Yet even if one agrees that *Waiting for Godot* is not
allegorical in the sense that events and characters relate
overall to specific external systems of thought and belief
(classical myth, Christianity, Cartesian philosophy, Hegelian-
ism, Marxism, or existentialism), there is no doubt that the
details and shape of the work itself keep forcing us to
generalize about its significance. The major questions then
become these: how and to what purpose *is* Beckett using
Christianity and other systems of beliefs and ideas 'as
mythology'? What if any generalizations can be reliably made
about a work that is so cunningly shaped to subvert general-
ization and to avoid definition?

At this point it is helpful to go back to Beckett's own
insistence that *Waiting for Godot* is designed to give artistic
expression to 'the irrational state of unknowingness wherein
we exist, this mental weightlessness which is beyond reason'.
Following this lead, it would be advantageous to begin talking
about the play not as a structure of ideas, but as the
dramatization of what it is like and what it means to exist in
a state of radical unknowingness. Approached in this way,
the situation in which the characters find themselves and how
they respond moment by moment in gesture and dialogue are

more absorbing and suggestive than any overall 'meaning' that can be formulated in discursive terms. This is not to deny the importance of ideas in the play (as we shall soon see), but rather to confirm Hugh Kenner's observation that a Beckett play contains ideas but that no idea contains the play.

The caged dynamic

Beckett dramatizes doubt and unknowingness in countless ways. When *Godot* opens, the accustomed contours of realistic theatre have already been thoroughly eroded, and much that we might expect to be told about the characters and their situation is denied to us. Where are these people, and who are they? What are they doing, and why? Although the protagonists have been identified in the cast list of characters as Vladimir and Estragon, they later call each other Didi and Gogo and answer to other names as well; and in any case, what are we to make of names so atypical and unfamiliar, and so teasing? Shabbily dressed, they appear uprooted, but are they tramps? And if so, where did they get their bowler hats? Joined now, how long have they been apart; indeed, how often and how long have they been together? Who's been beating Estragon and for what reason? Why are they alternately so exhausted, gloomy, irritable, admiring, cheerful, hurt, angry (all pointed words that are in Beckett's early stage directions)? So thoroughgoing is the erosion of certainty that one feels as if he or she has entered a dreamlike environment, and like all dreams this one is governed more by deep feeling than logic. The emotions expressed, though, are far in excess of any evidence available to account for them, and at the start all we can do is wonder.

As soon as the two men begin talking, the aural texture of the play becomes whimsically strange and in a surprising way even captivating. When he can't get his boot off, the frustrated Estragon says 'Nothing to be done', a conclusive admission of defeat that the ruminating Vladimir instantly relates to his condition on earth: 'all my life I've tried to put it from me . . .' Comically queer as it may seem, this exchange sets the note for what will soon emerge as a dominant rhythm of the play. There is to be no separation at all between the mundane and the lofty in *Waiting for Godot*. Common talk of boots and hats, of eating, of peeing or buttoning one's fly, of feeling pain, goes on simultaneously with dialogue about the nature of existence: of solitude and desire, disappointment and grief, of hope deferred and fulfillment (perhaps even salvation) longed for.

The increasing incongruity that marks this yoking of the physical and the spiritual, the low and the high, the comic and the serious intensifies the strangeness and in turn is intensified by everything else that occurs in the opening minutes of the play. When Vladimir acknowledges his friend's presence ('So there you are again'), Estragon answers 'Am I?', an amusing yet oddly ontological response that subverts the solidity of presence and further feeds our doubt about the 'reality' of this dramatic situation. Eager to celebrate their reunion, Vladimir says 'Get up till I embrace you', another curious locution that becomes no less peculiar when one is informed that it is an 'Irishism'.

Absence, then, (of a substantial physical world, solid facts, logical explanations) is palpable at the start; and what is not there seems potentially more meaningful than what is. In this context, silence — the things not said, the pauses between words and lines — takes on an eerie significance. 'Silence', Beckett once said, 'pours into this play like water into a sinking ship.' And on another occasion (when Barney Rosset was preparing the Grove Press edition of the play), Beckett suggested for the jacket a photo taken at an early performance at Krefeld in Germany towards the close of Act I: Vladimir drawing Estragon towards the wings, against the background of the moon and the tree. 'It *is* the play and would make a remarkable cover for your book', he told Rosset. 'All very spectral' he later said. Palpable, too, is a persistent anxiety about presence, a feeling that being itself is unnervingly mysterious, that life is resistent, precarious, sometimes sinister, and ultimately unfathomable: boots won't come off, people can't be known, shadowy figures beat one at night, one doesn't know why, and there is nothing to be done.

The withdrawal of traditional coherence and meaning and the heightened apprehension of absence, then, is the 'given' in *Waiting for Godot*, and everything that occurs in the play is conditioned and coloured by it. But if the bizarre atmosphere and the tone at the start suggest ghostliness, deprivation, and an accelerating distress, there is also operating from the first moments a surprisingly inspiriting counterforce. For every note suggesting bafflement, nullity or unease, there is a comment, a gesture or a conveyed emotion that delicately and often humorously resists and modifies the negative. Estragon's 'nothing to be done' (which will become a recurring motif in the play) can and should be read as an active as well as a passive utterance. 'Nothing' will be performed, executed, accomplished on the stage for the next two hours; we will witness what human beings can do when confronted by nothing. In fact, every time this phrase and others like it are spoken, something is immediately said or done to contradict finality and to open up again new and unexpected possibilities for thought and feeling.

Directing his renowned production of *Waiting for Godot* at the Schiller Theater in Berlin in 1975, Beckett noted that the tempo he wished to achieve at the outset was of 'a caged dynamic', an oxymoronic phrase that handsomely catches the clashing elements in the emerging rhythm of the play. The concept has a quite literal but also a larger metaphorical dimension. Concretely, it refers to the way the restless Vladimir and the sluggish Estragon move on stage, perpetually separating and coming back together, in meticulously choreographed sequences that give the play much of its balletic quality. But Vladimir and Estragon, like all human beings, exist in other sets of circles: living organisms subject to the cycles of time, on a round planet, orbiting the sun. Within the cage of that circle their possibilities are limited. They have been born, they will live for a term and then die; but at the same time that they acknowledge these facts they resist them by recreating and asserting meaning in the face of the fundamental negative constraints that define their condition. Much of the fascination — in truth the enchantment —

of *Waiting for Godot* arises from this basic dramatic (and human) tension, an active energy to which most people who find the play boring or static are failing to respond. Although the entire play is framed by the static situation of waiting, what goes on 'in the meanwhile' – when presence is enacted – has great variety and richness. (It is interesting to learn from the *Director's Notebook* Beckett kept in Berlin that he had contemplated at one point having a faint shadow of bars on the stage floor but finally dismissed the idea as overly explicit.)

It would, however, be platitudinous and certainly too solemn to continue in this vein and insist that the extractable theme of *Waiting for Godot* has to do with the experience of vacancy and the reconstitution of meaning in the present. The play is a theatrical representation of this fact, not a statement (or a series of statements) about it. To dramatize perceptions about meaninglessness and asserted signification, Beckett creates a fine-grained philosophical variety show, using techniques more commonly associated with music, dance, and such popular forms as vaudeville, cabaret, pantomime and the circus than with those of traditional theatre. He does not develop themes by creating a linear plot governed by demonstrable cause and effect; nor does he present characters whose impulses and motivations are probed or whose changing perceptions reveal the meaning of their lives and the larger import of the entire action.

Instead, Beckett proceeds by locating sources of drama elsewhere: in the markedly stylized talk and movements of his indefatigably waiting protagonists. He invents and builds up essentially anti-discursive blocks and units of speech and gesture, rituals and routines that (in Wallace Stevens' formulation) 'resist the intelligence, almost successfully' and yet carry forward the emotional and intellectual implications of the basic situation. A brilliant early illustration of the process occurs in the exchange that begins with Vladimir asking Estragon 'What are you doing?'

ESTRAGON: Taking off my boot. Did that never happen to you?
VLADIMIR: Boots must be taken off every day. I'm tired telling you that. Why don't you listen to me?

ESTRAGON: (*feebly*). Help me!
VLADIMIR: hurts?
ESTRAGON: Hurts! He wants to know if it hurts!
VLADIMIR: (*angrily*). No one ever suffers but you. I don't count.
          I'd like to hear what you'd say if you had what I have.
ESTRAGON: It hurts?
VLADIMIR: Hurts! He wants to know if it hurts!
ESTRAGON: (*pointing*). You might button it all the same.
VLADIMIR: (*stooping*). True. (*He buttons his fly.*) Never neglect
          the little things of life.
ESTRAGON: What do you expect, you always wait till the last
          moment.
VLAIMIR: (*musingly*). The last moment . . . (*He meditates.*)
          Hope deferred maketh the something sick, who said
          that?
ESTRAGON: Why don't you help me?   (F, 10; G, 7–8)

On its face the subject of this conversation is the everyday
predicament of people feeling pain and wishing for solace and
sympathy. The shape of the dialogue, however, is reminiscent
of the delightful comic turns that occur in a circus or music hall
number when two clowns perform a deft and wistfully funny
set of variations on a universal theme. Although the urgency of
the discomfort is paramount, the cadenced, almost lilting
repetition of the word 'hurts', and each man's deadpan refusal
to reveal if he knows that he is playing a verbal game, creates
the effect of ingenious artifice. The repartee admits the twinges
of pain and transforms them into something else: a brisk sparr-
ing match that elicits a smile and an affectionate nod of
recognition about human vulnerability and self-absorption.
One can understand from this scene (as well as from the entire
play) why Roger Blin once described his dream cast as Charlie
Chaplin for Vladimir, Buster Keaton for Estragon, and
Charles Laughton for Pozzo.

Like so many of the other set pieces, however, this one also
contains the elements that provide an unexpected transition to
a different level of discourse. When Estragon points to
Vladimir's unbuttoned fly and his friend sententiously says
'never neglect the little things of life', they are playing still
another variation on two of the oldest and most familiar jokes
about the laughable limits of human sexuality. But Estragon's

casual remark 'you always wait till the last moment' stirs the meditative Vladimir unsuccessfully to recall the full text from Proverbs 13, xii: 'Hope deferred maketh the heart sick, but when the desire cometh it is a tree of life', (which Beckett once said he did *not* have in mind when he translated from the French, but which a good many English-speaking spectators staring at the withered tree are likely to be thinking about).

Again, in a play where two clownish vagabonds spend all their time in front of a tree that is at first bare and then suddenly leaved, hoping for a meeting with someone who may save them, this dialogue certainly raises expectations. Yet when Estragon ignores the comment and Vladimir spins off into a different set of thoughts, the portentousness of the fragmented quotation appears to be undercut. Even so, there remains still another more fruitful way to think about its signifying function at this point, and also about the way similar allusions tend to evolve throughout the play.

So far we have been emphasizing the way the audience is seductively drawn into the stripped and alien environment of *Waiting for Godot*, where most of the assumptions of ordinary life and the manner in which it is customarily represented in the theatre are altered or reversed. Yet much of the appeal and force of the play comes from our realization that if this peculiar dreamworld is foreign, it is also in essential ways recognisably *our* world. One especially potent way in which this is true is that the action seems to be taking place at some transitional point in modern history when many old customs, references and beliefs are residual, existing only in fragments and without the power to give form and coherence to human lives. When Vladimir asks who said 'hope deferred maketh the something sick?' he is not alluding to the Bible as a book on which the spiritual life of an entire community rests, but is responding to the phrase as a vestige, a scrap he only half recalls and is intrigued by.

Although all the religious and literary allusions in *Waiting for Godot* are similarly traces — the surviving marks of former civilizations that may once have existed on the barren spot where the two men now wait — they nonetheless have ample power to command attention, inspire uneasiness and arouse hope, if not reverence. The most notable instance of this is the much discussed passage about the two thieves that occurs right after a nimbly choreographed scene featuring Vladimir staring into his hat and Estragon into his newly removed boot. Having just pontificated on the nature of man (a creature who blames on his boots the faults of his feet), Vladimir out of the blue says, 'One of the thieves was saved', pauses, and concludes, 'It's a reasonable percentage.' Understandably enough, Estragon asks 'what?', and so might a typical spectator or reader.

Thinking aloud and making no allowances for a listener, Vladimir runs on about the possibility of repentance, but when his friend asks what exactly they might feel contrite about, he casually insists that they wouldn't have to go into detail. A step ahead of him for a moment, Estragon queries 'Our being born?', a proposition that draws forth from Vladimir a hearty laugh which he quickly stifles, pressing his hand to his genitals and contorting his face. Here again the mix of the physical and the spiritual is unusually evocative. Earlier the audience had seen Vladimir walking with short, stiff strides, legs wide apart; and here one notes that laughing can cause him sharp discomfort. Ergo, he must have a problem urinating, an ailment painful to the individual and likely to be the source of humour to others. (Vladimir probably suffers from strangury, a condition in which urine is emitted painfully drop by drop – which would account for his awkward way of walking and his frequent need to pass water.)

The difficulty of laughing, though, is given broader application:

VLADIMIR: One daren't even laugh any more.
ESTRAGON: Dreadful privation.
VLADIMIR: Merely smile. (*He smiles suddenly from ear to ear, keeps smiling, ceases as suddenly.*) It's not the same thing. Nothing to be done. (*Pause.*) Gogo.
ESTRAGON: (*irritably*). What is it?
VLADIMIR: Did you ever read the Bible?

(F, 11–12; G, 8+)

Vladimir laughed originally at the prospect of trying to repent one's having been born, an obvious contradiction in terms if one believes in original sin. Here, though, laughter becomes a mode of expression that for an unstated reason isn't permitted any more. Only smiles are allowed, and they are not the same thing, the implication being that the situation in which the two men now find themselves is too serious a matter for laughter, while smiling is too modest a response to the dilemma. Extending the quirky logic of this a bit further, we end up perceiving that the situation of Vladimir and Estragon, might justifiably call for a more substantial response, and that in fact is what Vladimir is leading up to.

His subsequent gloss on the story of the two thieves takes as its main text the account of the crucifixion in *Luke* 23: 32–43, the most pertinent passage of which reads as follows:

One of the criminals who were hanged railed at him, saying 'Are you not the Christ? Save yourself and us!' But the other rebuked him, saying, 'Do you not fear God, since you are under the same sentence of condemnation? And we indeed justly; for we are receiving the due reward of our deeds; but this man has done nothing wrong.' And he said, 'Jesus, remember me when you come into your kingdom.' And he said to him, 'Truly, I say to you, today you will be with me in Paradise.'

What obsesses Vladimir is that this version is the only one of the four Gospel accounts in which the Evangelist speaks of a thief being saved. 'Of the other three two don't mention any thieves at all and the third says that both of them abused him.' So for Vladimir the story of the two thieves presents in bold form a disturbing problem of verification, and it is clear from his tone and attitude that issues of great consequence – matters of sin, guilt, salvation, and damnation – are at stake. For Estragon, though, Vladimir's brief foray into the higher criticism is something else again. Afflicted by his swollen foot, he can hardly care less for his friend's disquisition, and when pressed to 'return the ball, can't you, once in a way', has to force himself to feign enthusiasm and interest. As usual, though, the challenge of the game quickly becomes irresistible and the ensuing dialogue moves with the speed of a splendid rally in a tennis match.

VLADIMIR: One out of four. Of the other three two don't mention any thieves at all and the third says that both of them abused him.
ESTRAGON: Who?
VLADIMIR: What?
ESTRAGON: What's all this about? Abused who?
VLADIMIR: The Saviour.
ESTRAGON: Why?
VLADIMIR: Because he wouldn't save them.
ESTRAGON: From hell?
VLADIMIR: Imbecile! From death.
ESTRAGON: I thought you said hell.
VLADIMIR: From death, from death.
ESTRAGON: Well what of it?
VLADIMIR: Then the two of them must have been damned.
ESTRAGON: And why not?
VLADIMIR: But one of the four says that one of the two was saved.
ESTRAGON: Well? They don't agree and that's all there is to it.
VLADIMIR: But all four were there. And only one speaks of a thief being saved. Why believe him rather than the others?
ESTRAGON: Who believes him?
VLADIMIR: Everybody. It's the only version they know.
ESTRAGON: People are bloody ignorant apes.

The swiftness and lapidary quality of this dialogue paradoxically enhances both the seriousness and the comedy of what is being said. The seriousness resides not only in the subject-matter and the momentous issues at stake, but also in the particular form of the exchange, an imitation of the familiar stichomythic verse of Greek drama. In this kind of theatrical dialogue, two characters speak passionately and sometimes contentiously in alternate lines of verse. Each repeats and echoes some of his opponent's words, and the sharp retorts are part of a stylized format for debate in which one speaker tries to gain an advantage over the other. Here, however, as it often is in Beckett, the conclusion is comically, even explosively, inconclusive, spreading doubt further in every direction; and yet, despite the subversion, the most serious points continue to be made.

In addition to heightening the sense of anxious perplexity about questions that are gathering increased significance, this

laconic, witty exchange also provides cameo sketches of the
two men. Although Vladimir and Estragon are never
characterized in traditional ways (we know virtually nothing
about their histories or inner lives), they do have distinct personalities. Usually played by a short, stocky actor, Estragon
(in Beckett's formulation) is on the ground and belongs to the
stone. (Although the English text of the play describes
Estragon sitting on a low mound, Beckett in performance
prefers a stone, so that with the tree and the human beings,
animal, mineral, and vegetable would all be present on stage
from the start.) Estragon is the more dreamy, instinctive man,
absorbed by his own bodily functions and likely to respond
viscerally to everything going on around him. As his friend
ponders what may have happened on that fated day at
Calvary, Estragon behaves as if he were actually involved in
the crucifixion rather than merely thinking about it. In contrast, Vladimir is the more contemplative of the pair, self-
conscious about issues and ideas, just a bit of an exegete or
a scholastic philosopher, yet he is also more restless and
peripatetic than his stolid companion. 'Vladimir is light,'
Beckett once observed, 'he is oriented towards the sky. He
belongs to the tree.' Convention now dictates that the actor
playing this part be tall and thin, so that he might be thought
of as reaching for the sky, mirroring the tree.

   Given these traits, and denied many others that might par-
ticularize the two men, playgoers and readers have frequently
seen the naive and knowing figures as halves of some whole:
complementary friends, individuals in a marriage, poles of a
mind/body dichotomy, or figures who are associated with
and may even connect the earth and the sky. Sometimes (most
notably in Beckett's own Schiller Theater production) they
are dressed to suggest that each supplies what is lacking in the
other to make a complete whole, the way comedians in
vaudeville or Laurel and Hardy often do. Vladimir may wear
striped trousers, which fit well, and a black jacket, which is
too small for him, because it had once belonged to Estragon.
Estragon wears well-fitting black trousers, and Vladimir's old
striped jacket, which is too big for him.

To imagine the men as counterparts is reasonable, especially in the context of Beckett's often-quoted comment on the exchange about the thieves. Shortly after the English première of *Waiting for Godot*, the critic Harold Hobson told the playwright that people in London were vigorously arguing about the meaning of the new play, and Beckett wrote back:

I take no sides about that . . . I am interested in the shape of ideas even if I do not believe in them. There is a wonderful sentence in Augustine. I wish I could remember the Latin. It is even finer in Latin than in English. 'Do not despair; one of the thieves was saved. Do not presume; one of the thieves was damned.' That sentence has a wonderful shape. It is the shape that matters. (Hobson, p. 154)

This observation is often sensibly used to support the argument that Beckett is less interested in the truth value of ideas than in the aesthetic formulation of dichotomies. At issue for him is not so much the question of whether a thief was actually saved or damned but rather the perception that dualities are at the heart of what human beings think and feel, and the artist's concern about how they might be most vividly and suggestively expressed. In this regard, then, the pairings that many people think of when they encounter Vladimir and Estragon are persuasive and valuable. *Waiting for Godot* is very much a play about relationships, and the men *are* at different times two halves of a couple: married, single, external, internal, separating, and coming back together; and when, later in the action, Vladimir asserts that 'at this place, at this moment of time, all mankind is us, whether we like it or not', he is, despite the humorous pomposity of his formulation, quite right.

Rituals and routines

The basic structural unit of the play, then, is a self-contained routine or ritual in which our dichotomous couple blends the cross-talk and stylish patter of the vaudeville and music hall with the speculative vocabulary of philosophical discourse. But if each routine stands sturdily by itself, each is related to the others by what might be called the principle of accrual, rather than by the more familiar theatrical patterns of progressive plot, developing character, or the rise and fall of an action featuring a notable climax or denouement.

In the first act, for instance, every routine starts with a brief pantomime; indeed, this is the distinctive demarcation separating the discrete units. To open, the panting Estragon is seen sitting on the low mound trying several times unsuccessfully to take off his boot. Minutes later, after the introductory greetings, the brief clash about pain, and Estragon's surprising success in removing the boot, Vladimir silently engages in a meticulous inspection of the inside of his hat. A third routine − following the exchange about the two thieves − begins with Estragon in pain limping off to the left and then far right of the stage to gaze longingly into the distance, as Vladimir peers into his friend's boot and disgustedly recoils from the smell.

These scrupulously executed pantomimic sequences establish immediately the basic physical reality of the action: human beings are first seen in immediate relation to primary objects and sensory stimuli − hats and boots, what they look like and how they smell, whether or not they fit. The little dumb show also suggests that feeling comes before language: dialogue exists on the foundation of a prior visual and visceral perception of experience. And in Beckett's hands, pantomime is not only a basic strategy for expressing the silence of which the world is made, but also for dramatizing the disquiet of the isolated, suffering individual, who is a creature of that silence before he ever makes a gesture or utters a word, as he will be again when the gestures and the words are over. In addition, each early silent episode is a graphic vignette announcing a paramount theme of the play: man struggling against despair, man thinking about thinking, man dejected in his solitude, man looking for consolation in his abandonment. But if soundless gestures are existential signs, they are also (at least at the start) invitations to smile. Vladimir scrutinizing his bowler, or Gogo's boot; Estragon moving his arms like a spectator at a boxing match to encourage Didi peeing in the distance − these homely actions bring the men endearingly close to us at the same time that they confirm just how dejected and inscrutable they actually are.

Related to these opening pantomimes, indeed integral to them and to the dialogue that follows, are visual tableaux in which the silent action freezes into a striking scene. Like the pantomime, the tableau serves many purposes at once: to remind us of the primacy of the physical world and the silence that infuses it, but also to present a graphic representation of some of the play's major themes. When Beckett directed *Waiting for Godot* in Berlin, he told the actors that it should be done very simply and that the essential aim was 'to give confusion a shape . . . through the visual repetition of themes. Not only themes in the dialogue, but also visual themes of the body.' To illustrate his point, he chose the initial tableau of Estragon asleep on the stone and called this a *Wartestelle*, a 'waiting point' or 'a fixed moment of stillness, where everything stands completely still and silence threatens to swallow everything up. Then the action starts again' (reported by his associate director Walter Asmus in *Theatre Quarterly*, 1975).

First pantomime and tableau, then speech. Each unit in Act I of the play follows an expressive visual action with a conversational exchange that first asserts something concrete about the literal situation and then immediately dissolves that solidity with corrosive dialogue that comes so quickly in its wake. In the first routine, for instance, after the mute Vladimir spits in disgust at the smell of Estragon's boot, his friend moves to the centre of the stage, halts with his back to the audience, and addresses a comment to the landscape: 'Charming spot.' Given the denuded scene and the destitution of the characters, every playgoer will smile comfortably at the broad irony here, but what then happens complicates matters considerably. Estragon turns, walks to the front of the stage, faces the audience, and continues: 'Inspiring prospects' − and turning to Vladimir − says 'Let's go.'

VLADIMIR: We can't.
ESTRAGON: Why not?

VLADIMIR: We're waiting for Godot.
ESTRAGON: (*despairingly*). Ah! (Pause.)
                You're sure it was here?   (F, 14; G, 10)

On one hand, we are given vital specific information: these two seedy men are waiting for someone named Godot, and Estragon's tone suggests the possibility that they have done it before and had been disappointed. (In productions that Beckett directed in Berlin and London in 1975 and 1984, the actor playing Estragon said 'Ah, yes!' instead of merely 'Ah!' which confirms the sense of familiarity and frustrated expectation.) But the joke aimed at the audience quickly subverts our confidence that we know the difference between illusion and reality, a subversion that becomes increasingly more radical as the play goes on. Also more severe are subsequent comments directed at the spectators, who later on are compared as a group to a bog and as individuals to corpses and skeletons.

The conversation immediately following the first mention of Godot withdraws any comfort that might have existed in the original assertion about waiting. One man says something that he hopes the other will confirm, only to have his friend cast doubt on whatever slim hope he had originally expressed. When Estragon is told that they were supposed to meet Godot near the tree, he asks what kind of tree it is:

VLADIMIR: I don't know. A willow.
ESTRAGON: Where are the leaves?
VLADIMIR: It must be dead.
ESTRAGON: No more weeping.
VLADIMIR: Or perhaps it's not the season.
ESTRAGON: Looks to me more like a bush.
VLADIMIR: A shrub.
ESTRAGON: A bush.
VLADIMIR: A—. What are you insinuating? That we've come to
                the wrong place?   (F, 14: G, 10)

Vladimir's 'I don't know. A willow' is a classic instance of Beckett's way of simultaneously asserting and withdrawing meaning, and its effect is to characterize Vladimir as an honest doubter in search of certainty, a man caught between ignorance and a need to know. In one respect, the willow is only a willow, but in another it functions as what Antonin Artaud once called 'an animated hieroglyphic'. Because of their drooping leaves and frequent location near water, willows are often associated with grief for unrequited love or the loss of a mate. Vladimir's assertion that the willow must be dead and Estragon's attempt to put an end to weeping appear a conclusive enough effort to get beyond one kind of loss; but the unexpected addition about the possibility that this perhaps is not the season for willows, or that the willow may not in fact be a willow at all, puts the suspicion of doubt about Godot in yet a different and even more unnerving context.

Literally, then, space is questioned: this may not be the place where they are to meet Godot. And then time comes in for its relentless cross-examination:

ESTRAGON: And if he doesn't come?
VLADIMIR: We'll come back tomorrow.
ESTRAGON: And then the day after tomorrow.
VLADIMIR: Possibly.
ESTRAGON: And so on.
VLADIMIR: The point is –
ESTRAGON: Until he comes.
VLADIMIR: You're merciless.
ESTRAGON: We came here yesterday.
VLADIMIR: Ah no, there you're mistaken.
ESTRAGON: What did we do yesterday?
VLADIMIR: What did we do yesterday?
ESTRAGON: Yes.
VLADIMIR: Why . . . (*Angrily*). Nothing is certain when you're
              about.   (F, 14, G, 10+)

By raising the possibility that Godot may not come, Estragon prompts Vladimir to affirm their steadfastness, but he needs only to project the forced affirmation one day into the future to reveal its shakiness and to nudge his friend into the weaker 'possibly'. And if tomorrow is uncertain, yesterday turns out to be more so: not only are they unable to agree that they were here a day earlier, but they cannot remember what they *did* then. With the future and the past so decisively thrown into question, the only thing that seems to retain its solidity is the present. But when Vladimir concludes 'Nothing is certain when you're about', his cunning word play reminds his friend and us that the present, too, rests on a precarious foundation. By the end of this routine about the instability of space and time, the persistent scepticism of Vladimir and Estragon has evolved through elegantly executed sticho-mythic dialogue into serious farce and then into agitation and panic, prompting the weary Estragon to call for a truce by asking if they might 'stop talking for a while, do you mind?'

But to stop talking is to succumb to the silence and the fourth major routine of the first act begins with a pantomime in which Estragon, having sat down on his mound, drifts off into sleep, while the alarmed Vladimir paces back and forth stopping only to stare off into the distance as if looking for relief. Unable to bear the cessation of speech, he cries out 'Gogo! . . . Gogo! . . . GOGO!' to wake his friend up. Estragon, 'restored to the horror of his situation', wants to escape by narrating a dream he has just had, but Vladimir in his agitation won't listen, a refusal that elicits from Estragon a sweeping gesture towards the universe and the plangent question: 'This one is enough for you?'

What follows is a stylish variation on a by now familiar response. Estragon wonders if it might not be better for them to part, and to Vladimir's disdainful 'You wouldn't go far' he sarcastically answers: 'That would be too bad, really too bad . . . When you think of the beauty of the way. And the goodness of the wayfarers. Wouldn't it, Didi?' Estragon's needling, ironical use of a language with biblical overtones continues to give to the mundane talk a resonance that serves (as much else does here) to expand the emotional range and thematic implications and to introduce new images and motifs that will be repeated and developed later on.

At this point, a truncated anecdote works in a similar way. As their dispute heats up, Vladimir urges his friend to calm himself; and Estragon playfully picks up the word 'calm', strokes it, and asks Vladimir if he knows the story of the Englishmen in the brothel. The exchange that follows has all the marks of an age-old vaudeville routine. When Vladimir admits he knows the story, Estragon teasingly says 'Tell it to me', but when his friend protests at having been guyed,

Estragon nonchalantly begins to recount it himself: an intoxicated Englishman goes to a brothel and the madam asks him if he wants 'a fair one, a dark one or a red-haired one'. Just then in the narration, with exquisite timing, Estragon asks his friend to 'go on', but the baited Vladimir shouts 'STOP IT', and heads off in a huff.

At this point one can make little more of the unfinished bawdy interlude, but the exchange about 'do you know the story . . . tell it to me' echoes Vladimir's introduction to the account of the two thieves; and Ruby Cohn reports that in the second act of Beckett's German production, when Vladimir asks the boy whether Mr Godot's beard is fair or black, the German question becomes 'Blonde or . . . (he hesitates) black . . . (he hesitates) . . . or red?' (The standard line in English reads 'Fair or . . . (he hesitates) . . . or black?') And Cohn then provides the text of the joke: An Englishman, having drunk a little more than usual, goes to a brothel. The bawd asks him if he wants a fair one, a dark one, or a red-haired one. The Englishman replies that he wants a boy. Shocked, the bawd threatens to call a policeman, and the Englishman pleads: 'Oh, no, they're too gritty.' In this way Godot is brought into relation to Gogo's coarse story, juxtaposing – as so often in Beckett's play – 'the physical and metaphysical, the vulgar and ethereal' (*Journal of Beckett Studies*, I (Winter 1976), p. 42, n. 2).

As revealing as this account is, there is no need to wait until the end of Act II to see how Estragon's bawdy story provides motifs for successive early sections of the play. The fifth substantial routine in the early part of Act I begins with a pantomime in which Estragon gestures to encourage the absent Vladimir peeing offstage. Reunited a few minutes later, the two men introduce their favorite topic – 'what do we do now' – and Estragon proposes that they should hang themselves. Vladimir is drawn to the idea because he knows from folklore (and perhaps from reading James Joyce's *Ulysses*) that hanged men often get erections. As Joyce has his Dubliner Alf Bergan explain:

– God's truth . . . I heard that from the head warder that was in Kilmainham when they hanged Joe Brady, the invincible. He told me when they cut him down after the drop it was standing up in their faces like a poker.

– Ruling passion strong in death, says Joe, as someone said.

– That can be explained by science, says Bloom. It's only a natural phenomenon . . . (*Ulysses*, Random House, New York, 1986, p. 250)

But hanging in Beckett never works out as neatly as it might in life or in other books. From friendship and a surprisingly refined sense of *noblesse oblige*, Vladimir and Estragon comically defer to one another and get entangled in a dispute about who is the heavier of the two. After another exchange reminiscent of a scene from a Marx-Brothers movie, Estragon uncharacteristically gets the better of the argument and suggests they do nothing, because 'it's safer'.

VLADIMIR: Let's wait and see what he says.
ESTRAGON: Who?
VLADIMIR: Godot.
ESTRAGON: Good idea.   (F, 18; G, 12+)

'Godet . . . Godot . . . Godin . . . anyhow you see who I mean?'

The exchange that follows is the first prolonged discussion about the mysterious figure for whom Vladimir and Estragon spend the entire play waiting. From this solemn, antiphonal conversation, Godot emerges as someone who appears to have considerable respectability and power in his community. Said to be surrounded by the trappings of commercial success (correspondents, books, bank accounts, agents, a family and confortable home), he is invested with the authority to set the time, place, and terms of their appointment, and to make the two indigents look forward eagerly to what he has to offer. Vladimir claims they have met him before and had asked at that time for 'nothing very definite', expressing their desires 'as a kind of prayer . . . a vague supplication'. This devotional vocabulary is soon intensified by mention of the wind in the reeds (a phrase used by Jesus to refer to the Messianic herald, John, not recognized by the multitudes) and by

Vladimir's portentous answer to the question 'Where do we come in?' – 'On our hands and knees'.

At the start, then, Godot exists entirely as a creature perceived in all earnestness by Vladimir and Estragon, and they clearly associate him with concrete images of authority and with less concrete but nonetheless provocative images suggesting divinity – as someone who can certainly do 'something' for them. As Kristin Morrison has helpfully noted, 'the wind in the reeds' literally means 'there is nothing', but 'through its biblical reference the lines suggest that once there was something or someone who went unrecognized and that those who awaited but did not detect him were not saved' (Morrison, p. 20).

Yet equally early on, as the two men talk about the figure they are waiting to meet, these images of authority and divinity, of promises and expectations, become increasingly more cloudy and difficult to interpret. While he is feasting on Vladimir's carrot, Estragon reintroduces the subject of whether they are tied to 'your man Godot', and Vladimir adopts again the verbal habit of simultaneously asserting and withdrawing meaning that is one of the dominant stylistic features of the entire play. Dismissive at first, he says 'No question of it', but after a portentous '(*Pause*.)' he replies: 'For the moment.' And when Estragon asks 'His name is Godot?', Vladimir says 'I think so.'

The clamorous arrival of the fearsome landowner and his servant spreads confusion even further. The fuddled Estragon, who is supposed to have previously met Godot, mistakes Pozzo for the man they're waiting for, and after the comical game of 'get the name wrong', Pozzo begins a stern interrogation that discloses how little Vladimir and Estragon can actually say for certain about the enigmatic figure of Godot.

POZZO: (*peremptory*). Who is Godot?
ESTRAGON: Godot?
POZZO: You took me for Godot.
VLADIMIR: Oh no, sir, not for an instant, sir.
POZZO: Who is he?

VLADIMIR: Oh, he's a . . . he's a kind of acquaintance.
ESTRAGON: Nothing of the kind, we hardly know him.
VLADIMIR: True . . . we don't know him very well . . . but all the same . . .
ESTRAGON: Personally I wouldn't even know him if I saw him.
POZZO: You took me for him.
ESTRAGON: (*recoiling before Pozzo*). That's to say . . . you understand . . . the dusk . . . the strain . . . waiting . . . I confess . . . I imagined . . . for a second . . .

(F, 23; G, 16)

What began moments earlier as comedy starts turning grave here, but not for long. Pozzo soon loses interest in the subject of Godot and the two friends become increasingly absorbed by the novel and violent antics of the master and his woebegone servant. For a long stretch of time, everyone pretty much forgets about Godot (except for Pozzo, who twice menacingly asks what would happen if Vladimir and Estragon did *not* stay for their appointment 'with this . . . Godet . . . Godot . . . Godin . . . anyhow you see who I mean, who has your future in his hands . . . (pause) . . . at least your immediate future?').

The effect of this extraordinary mixture of outlandish farce and illogical, contradictory, and self-cancelling rhetoric is gradually to remove the question 'who is Godot?' from the realm of ordinary discourse. By this time in the action it should be clear that Godot can hardly be considered a figure in a realistic narrative, or even in a coherent allegory, both of which have been subverted or exploded at every point. Rather, for us at least if not for the two men on the road, Godot has become a concept – an idea of promise and expectation – of that for which people aware of the absence of coherent meaning in their lives wait in the hope that it will restore significance to their existence.

Waiting for Godot, then, is a play not about Godot – who he is or whether he will ever arrive – but about waiting; or, to be more precise, about what people do while they wait. In this regard, Beckett's French title, *En Attendant Godot*, *While Waiting for Godot*, is a more precise rendering than the title he gave to his English translation. Thoughts about the

interim, the provisional, what happens 'in the meantime' are
more relevant to the adventures of Vladimir and Estragon than
notions of termination, attainment, and closure. Approached
in this way, the play becomes a far richer and more suggestive
work than it would be if Godot were interpreted as a single,
definable entity; as God, for instance, or as a liberator from
some specific tyranny or exile (the Nazi occupation of France
or separation from one's homeland).

But there is yet another way in which Godot has come to
exist both inside and outside Beckett's play. As Colin
Duckworth has usefully observed, the name itself 'is a
trouvaille of the first order', a lucky find or a godsend, 'opening up several associations of ideas, through punning and
analogy, in both English and French'. Beckett appears to
have been fascinated from adolescence by words in foreign
languages that have the English letters g-o-d in them. In one
respect this sustained interest is obviously playful, the kind of
enjoyment that anyone sensitive to words would get from verbal coincidences, and evidence of the pleasure Beckett takes
in such yokings is apparent everywhere in the text. Yet a
delight in chance correspondences is only the beginning.

Of a dozen common French words and phrases that begin
with g-o-d, nearly every one has some teasing connection to
the story and theme of Beckett's play. *Godillot* is French for
'hobnailed boot' or 'shapeless old shoe'; and *godasses* are
'military boots'. *Godailler* is 'to go pub-crawling', and *god-
dam* is French slang for 'an Englishman' (who according to
Estragon had drunk a little more than usual on the way to the
brothel). *Goder* means 'to pucker', or 'gather cloth into
folds', but it is also slang for having an erection. *Godiller*, the
word for 'a scull', or 'small racing boat', has a vulgar connotation: 'to fornicate'. And *godenot* is 'a juggler's puppet',
'a joker', 'a misshapen little man'.

Closest in sound is *godet*, the name of a popular cognac,
but also the French word for 'a wooden bowl' or 'mug',
which in different usages refers to the bowl of a pipe (smoked
by Pozzo who carelessly refers to Godot as Godet) and a
small glass of wine (which washes down Pozzo's chicken). In

the French original, Vladimir identifies Lucky's dance as 'la mort du lampiste', 'the death of the lamplighter'; and as Frederick Busi has helpfully noted, a lamplighter is the person charged with keeping town lights illuminated, a job which used to require small receptacles called *godets* filled with combustible materials and wicks. Inevitably, as Colin Duckworth has concluded, the receptacle called a *godet* might in the broad sense hold any meaning put into it.

Pertinent, too, is the fact that in French to add the suffix '-ot' to the end of a word is to turn it into a diminutive, usually with an endearing connotation: to call a friend Jacquot or Jeannot is to express fond familiarity, and in France Charlie Chaplin's nickname is the affectionate Charlot. Thus to coin the name 'God-ot' is to invent a figure who might be thought of as 'an endearing little god', 'a minor god', but certainly not the Supreme Being, the creator and ruler of the universe. To move beyond French: 'Godo' is spoken Irish for God; 'Godin' is a walled plane in the first quadrant of the face of the moon, about twenty-seven miles in diameter; and so on, *ad infinitum*.

The ingenious comedy of all this teasing word play is obvious, but there are some important serious implications as well. To set off an endless chain of verbal correspondences, to demonstrate that 'g-o-d' is indeed everywhere in the physical and spiritual world, but is of disputed etymology, can never be made manifest in one entity and has no fixed meaning — all this is to create an image of extraordinary suggestiveness and contemporary applicability. In the literal terms of the plot, Godot is the man Vladimir and Estragon are waiting for on a country road and who does not come; but in the broader linguistic universe of Beckett's play (and indeed outside it), Godot becomes an absent person or object that human beings desire and for whom (or for which) they feel obliged to wait. Developing this figure throughout the play, Beckett — as Václav Havel has shrewdly said — juggles with the world.

Since Beckett's play opened in the winter of 1953, Godot has turned up with startling regularity in many different shapes and forms and is certain to keep turning up. In 1956, Eric Bentley reminded his readers that Balzac once wrote a theatre piece called *Mercadet* in which a financially strapped merchant waits for a business partner, Godeau, who never appears. Close to the final curtain, Godeau is reported to have come back enormously rich from India, and his alleged arrival saves the situation and assures a happy ending, but he never actually appears in the play. Bernard Dukore has pointed out that in *The Soldiers*, the best-known work of the eighteenth-century German playwright, Jakob Lenz, Godeau is a French actor-manager. A backnote in a recent English translation points out that 'there seems to be no record of any real person of that name'. Hugh Kenner recalls having been told by Beckett about a well-known French racing-cyclist, Godeau, and he recounts the anecdote of a crowd standing around at the end of a race. 'Qu'est-ce qu'on attend?' they were asked. 'On attend Godeau', one man answered. Ruby Cohn tells us that the French concern with the unity of time in drama begins in the seventeenth century with Jean Chapelain's 'Lettre sur la règle des vingt-quatre heures', addressed to Antoine Godeau. One might add to her observation that according to the *Oxford Companion to French Literature*, Godeau was an *habitué* of the Hôtel de Rambouillet, where owing to his diminutive stature he was known as Julie's dwarf (Julie being Mme de Rambouillet's daughter) and that among the literary works of the man who was to become Bishop of Grasse and Vence were both profane poems and sacred odes. Countless people have noted that not far from *l'Ecole normale supérieure* in Paris, where young Beckett taught as an exchange lecturer, is the Rue Godot de Mauroy, a street known for high-priced whores. And Beckett himself has told friends of the time he travelled to London by plane and was disconcerted to hear the pilot address the passengers over the loudspeaker: 'Le capitaine Godeau vous accorde des bienvenues.'

It has become commonplace for people who have seen or read *Waiting for Godot* to encounter the name in unexpected and often humorous contexts: on a billboard in California

(where it advertised a funeral parlour), on the radio in Poland
(where it referred to clashes between Solidarity and the
government), or on the campus of the University of Sierra
Leone (where it was the name of a student's vagrant cat).
Douglas Hofstadter, the author of the brilliant *Gödel,
Escher, Bach*, defines his ideal reader as 'a bright fifteen-
year-old who is interested in the kind of thing that interested
me when I was fifteen'. He had read *Waiting for Godot* at
that age and was fascinated by the fact that the first three letters of 'Godot' were the same (barring the umlaut) as the first
three letters of the name of the mathematician Gödel, whose
infuriatingly limitative theorem he had just discovered. Indeed, this kind of fascination with the title figure has carried
over to the entire play itself. The Irish actor Barry McGovern,
who has performed around the world in *I Can't Go On*, a
one-man show based on the *Trilogy*, considers himself blessed
to have been born on 17 November 1948. 'The dates of
Godot', he points out, 'are 9 October 1948 to 29 January
1949, so I always reckon I was born in the middle of Lucky's
speech.'

Whether Beckett knew of Balzac's *Mercadet* or the story of
the cyclist before he wrote *En attendant Godot* (he says he
didn't) is of little importance. What matters is the extraordinary network of endless verbal correspondences that link
the trivial and the profound, for ultimately this is where the
significance of his inspired naming and his intuitions about
human hope and waiting will continue to expand.

Pozzo and Lucky

Inside the play the significance of the enigmatic title figure
expands in different ways. Although the entering Pozzo is
reasonably mistaken for Godot (several traits make the error
plausible and in some ways tantalizing: the similar sounding
name, the trappings of authority, the fact that someone is
'tied' to him), he and Lucky import enough meaning by themselves. From the moment they appear, the bellowing master
and his shackled slave stand as contrasts to the impoverished

other couple and seem to embody much that is absent in their personalities and situation. If Vladimir and Estragon are defined by their tenuousness – by what they and we don't know of their histories and purpose, by the nervous questions they ask and the answers denied to them – Pozzo and Lucky announce themselves immediately as substantial creatures of context and direction.

The flamboyant master exudes force and authority; the encumbered servant fittingly displays a cowed submissiveness. 'I present myself: Pozzo . . . Made in God's image!' the whip-wielding figure says and then acts with an overbearing mix of callousness and civility that appears to reflect a thousand years of inherited rule. He brusquely quizzes the two strangers about Godot, is magnanimous when he learns of their trespassing on his land, and settles down ostentatiously to enjoy his dinner and his pipe. His speech is marked by imperatives, exclamations, and affected aphorisms, and he moves back and forth between bluster and elocutionary set pieces about the tears of the world and the ominous radiance of the local twilight that fascinate at the same time that they unnerve. The slave at the end of his rope fetches and carries on order, nearly swoons, but unlike Didi and Gogo never doubts his place.

Vladimir and Estragon are instantly diverted and terror-struck, drawn out of their worrisome waiting into the fabulous display of calculated self-presentation. *This* must be what the world outside is really like: all spectacle and surety and fixed purpose – a kind of consequential theatre. 'I am bringing him to the fair,' says Pozzo of Lucky, 'where I hope to get a good price for him.' With a histrionic show of such novelty and violence to absorb their attention, Didi and Gogo need not brood about keeping an appointment with Godot. But from the start Pozzo's performance is clearly *over*-determined, and his authority is quickly revealed to be imposed, factitious not genuine. His answer to Estragon's question about why Lucky doesn't put down his bags is a drawn-out parody of a logical explanation; his mannered outburst about the slave 'killing him' is more evidence of the emptiness of his own claims to power. One by one he misplaces his pipe, his atomizer, his precious watch — possessions associated with this sense of mastery.

Pozzo tries to recover his authority by playing the role of impresario and offering to do something to entertain 'these honest fellows who are having such a dull, dull time', but his offer to have Lucky dance or sing or recite turns out to be the invitation that exposes his own impotence and leads ultimately to his rout.

Lucky's 'think'

Lucky's astonishing tirade is the most graphic of all the rituals and routines in a play full of unforgettable set sequences. In the 1950s, when *Godot* was first performed around the world, the speech tended to be read as some sort of demented, show-stopping aria: a mix of gibberish, parody, and portentous symbolism. Gibberish because it was customarily delivered at such breakneck speed that it could not be comprehended by an audience (and remained unintelligible to a reader); parody because it was clearly a mocking version of a theological proof ('Given the existence of a personal God . . . therefore . . .'); and symbolic because the allusions to Shakespeare's *The Tempest*, to lyrics by Verlaine and Hölderlin, to Samuel Johnson (in the early British edition) and Bishop Berkeley (in the American) suggested that the torrent of fragments reflected an advanced stage in man's mechanical thinking about the collapse of Western civilization. All of this is essential, but more recently the speech has been interpreted as a far more formal and meaningful structure than it had been understood to be at the time the play first gained its fame (though no one would ever want to defuse its force as a mindboggling tirade by overemphasizing its coherence).

When Beckett directed *Godot* at the Schiller Theater in 1975, he surprisingly announced to the actors on the first day that rehearsals would begin with Lucky's speech, for it was here, he said, that the 'threads and themes' of the play 'are being gathered together'. He then proceeded to explain the movement of the piece in a way that clarifies its shape and significance. The monologue's theme, he told the cast, is 'to shrink on an impossible earth under an indifferent heaven', and it is divided into three parts: an apathetic divinity, dwindling man, and indifferent nature. Following Beckett's lead, one would want also to comment in some detail on the texture as well as the structure of what Lucky says to explain further why − unintelligible *and* intelligible − it is so central to an appreciation and understanding of the play.

At first, one is flabbergasted by Lucky's vehement harangue because it comes so surprisingly out of the silence: not only had he not spoken before, but he seemed a depraved creature incapable of any speech, let alone the speech he gives us. But then, from the mouth of this animal comes a panic-driven discourse on the nature of God and man in the universe that reproduces in its very movement the essential dramatic pressure of everything in the play that has preceded it. Lucky's convulsive attempt to begin by asserting the existence of 'a personal God' who 'loves us dearly with some exceptions for reasons unknown' parallels the ongoing efforts of Vladimir and Estragon to establish a meaningful presence in their own lives; and the forces of non-sense and negativity that confound his endeavor are very much like those that bedevil theirs.

But if their undertaking has been oddly, comically poignant, his is terrifying not only because of the delirium in which it is delivered but also because he is suddenly shown to carry so much intellectual baggage along with the paraphernalia he actually hauls about for Pozzo. Lucky is a grotesque likeness of scholarly man at the end of his tether, starting out to make a last-ditch effort, through all the erudition he can muster, to claim the largest coherence for human beings in the universe. Yet, although his speech at the start takes the form of the ancient philosophical proof of the existence of God, it hurtles immediately to different, frightful set of conclusions. The authorities on whose work his proof rests are a ticket-puncher and a tram-driver (Puncher and Wattmann); the God with the white beard (who loves us dearly for reasons unknown) is characterized by freedom from emotion, imperturbability, and the loss of the power to use spoken or written language (apathia, athambia, aphasia). The noise that seems involuntarily to puncture Lucky's proof ('quaquaquaqua') is related both to ultimate meaning and ultimate nonsense: 'qua' as 'essential being, in the character or capacity of . . .'; or 'quaquaversal', literally: 'wheresoever turned, turned everywhere, sloping downward from the centre in all directions' (which Beckett once called a divine attribute). But the staccato 'quaquaquaqua' sounds like the derisive noises made by Ovid's frogs and the nihilist Soliony when he wants to belittle and silence other people in Chekhov's *Three Sisters*.

As Lucky's desperation increases so does the scalding contempt directed at academies and academics, all named in coarsely dismissive ways: the Acacacacademy of Anthropopopometry of Essy-in-Possy is both excremental and sterile (*esse* = 'to be'; *posse* = 'to be able'; i.e. in this context, '*not* to be able to measure man'), and Testew, Cunard, Fartov, and Belcher speak for themselves. But if the diction is crude and convoluted and the manner pedantically prolix, the message is clear: if God exists, He is absent, unresponsive to us, and despite heralded strides in nutrition, personal hygiene, medicine, and communication, human beings waste and pine, shrink and dwindle.

Although Lucky's corrosively ironical, despairing thesis is stated at almost the exact middle of this seventy-two line speech, the second half is of equal importance, for not only does it complete the discourse about an indifferent nature complementing an apathetic God, but it introduces the essential (and in many ways startling) Beckett note of resistance. Just at the point when the argument is most chillingly apocalyptic (the vision of the fading human skull in the abode of stones), Lucky begins his two closing refrains: 'I resume' and 'on on . . .' explosive utterances − repeated half-a-dozen times in the second half of the speech, when they were not present at all in the first half. 'To resume': 'to take up or go on with again after interruption' − this is what Lucky does and what Vladimir and Estragon have been doing (and will continue to do) when they reconstitute a dying world by some purposive action or verbal excursion.

The interruption here, as it often is in Beckett's work, is an intrusion of some grim, unwelcome truth, an essential fact that has previously been excluded by the characters' propensity to live in the grip of habit and routine. 'Habit', Vladimir will tell us in his second-act soliloquy, is 'a great deadener', and Beckett invariably associates it with the human capacity for evasion and self-protection. Habit, he wrote at twenty-four in his essay on Proust, is a compromise effected between the individual and his environment, a 'guarantee of dull inviolability' against the explosive moments when 'the boredom of living is replaced by the suffering of being'.

Lucky's tirade is one such shattering interjection, and when he himself is violently silenced by Vladimir's pulling off his hat, the action returns to the world of habit to which we had earlier been accustomed – the circus world of extravagant theatricality with its insinuating reminders of events that are reported to have taken place at Calvary (Latin for 'skull') or Golgotha (Hebrew for 'skull'); or, in Lucky's terms: 'on on the skull the skull the skull the skull in Connemara . . .'

After Lucky falls, he is clumsily raised by the two friends in a farcical yet distressing parody of the crucifixion. (Pozzo's 'Raise him up' followed by Estragon's 'To hell with him'.) The reactions of the others can be taken as an index to the impact of Lucky's 'interruption'. Much of the force of the tirade comes from its having the finality of a savage obsession: no further discussion is possible. Not only does it expose Pozzo's authoritarian posturing, but it reminds Vladimir and Estragon of the grim terms and conditions of the world in which they have been waiting to keep their appointment with Godot. The shrill comedy of Pozzo's farewell – the skit about the misplaced watch, the ludicrous cross-cutting exchange of 'adieu . . . yes yes no no' – are forced efforts to evade the implications of Lucky's speech, a travesty of habit at the end of *its* tether.

After Pozzo and Lucky make their preposterous exit, the

emotional progression of the play takes another important turn. We find Vladimir and Estragon in a different mood
from that in which we saw them before the master/slave
spectacle occurred. The original entrance of Pozzo and Lucky
had notably increased the derelicts' sense of possibility: the big
man might be Godot; he could be bringing something to eat;
the antics of the travelling pair would be a longed-for diversion. But those illusions are gone the moment Didi and Gogo
are alone.

Now they seem even more conscious than before of the
desperation of their situation and of the theatrical aspect of
their own lives. Cast down by the departure of what was the
only show in town and by an intuition that the crazed Lucky
has accurately defined the conditions of the world in which
they exist, they start talking again about how to pass the time
while waiting for Godot. At this point, however, there is a
conversation that alters both the tone and the implications of
the action. Unexpectedly, Vladimir remarks 'How they've
changed!' and the dialogue that follows reveals the possibility
that the encounter with Pozzo and Lucky may have occurred
before – a disclosure that suddenly opens the earlier action
to a new range of interpretations. If, as now seems possible,
the two down-and-outers have been acting all along, slyly
playing dumb for reasons we can only begin to guess at, we
may be (as they are) even further into a world of mystery and
unknowingness than we had realized.

The effects of the revelation that much of this may have
occurred before are manifold. First, it further confounds the
audience about the meaning and implications of the action.
Secondly, it heightens the importance of the events of the play
as theatre, as the knowing imitation of actions that supposedly
have a reality elsewhere. And, finally, it accentuates the need
for the spectators and readers to concentrate more intently on
how Vladimir and Estragon respond to events – the way they
perform their roles – rather than on the significance of the
events overall.

As spectators and readers, we have been aware from early
on that in Beckett's dreamscape the logic of cause and effect

and of conventional explanation has broken down. But we have assumed, too, that for Didi and Gogo what has been happening on this country road *is* the real world, uncertain as they may be whether some of it happened before or not. Indeed, the improbable talk, the tedium and bizarre goings-on are as vividly actual for them as the occurrences and conversations of our daily lives are likely to be for us — yet all this repetition may be putting these goings-on in doubt.

Enter the Boy

That this confounding should take place just before the Boy enters is a brilliant theatrical stroke, for it is of course he who seems to be bringing the first external verification of the existence of Godot. But the undermining of any hold the audience might have on causation, connection, or general meaning has been so persistent that the only thing one can be confident of is the continued annulment of certainty in the present. And this in fact is not only what happens, but it also turns out to be what the scene is 'about': how Vladimir and Estragon continue to respond in the act of waiting to the frustration of expectation and the denial of certainty. As J. P. Little has observed, 'Godot as an existent being is of dubious reality, but their wait is the very fabric of their lives.'

Hearing the cry 'Mister', Vladimir is the more welcoming of the couple. He gently bids the Boy approach and when the disbelieving Estragon barks questions and commands, Vladimir tries to put the child at his ease and provides excuses for his being late. As the two men continue their criss-cross of ill-tempered questions and kindly defences, it becomes increasingly clear that their behaviour is designed less to get a direct answer about a message from Godot (which they seem to intuit will be negative) than to enact some agenda of their own. Estragon, hobbled again by an aching foot, expresses his frustration by the persistent hostility of his commands and questions; Vladimir, whose distress at the moment is less specific, is more concerned with establishing the solid facts of the present situation. He does ask the direct question early on, 'You have a message from Mr Godot?', but when Estragon breaks in to prevent the Boy's answer, his more philosophic friend accepts the distraction and gets involved in talk about the Boy's fear and Estragon's unhappiness.

Estragon's confession 'I'm unhappy' is another one of those startling moments when the 'boredom of living is replaced by the suffering of being'; and with his face convulsed, he tries to speak, gives up, and hobbles to his mound to nurse his aching feet (in the grip of habit once again). Vladimir's main concern in this sequence is to try to determine if he and the Boy had met yesterday; indeed, he butts in with 'I've seen you before, haven't I?' when the child utters only the two words 'Mr Godot—'. The Boy's insistence that this is his first errand disturbs the man more than the message he gets a moment later: that Godot won't come this evening but surely tomorrow. Vladimir greets the much-delayed report with the casual 'Is that all?' and proceeds to initiate a long exchange about the Boy's place in Mr Godot's employ. For the reflective Vladimir, the critical question seems not whether Godot will come (he intuits the answer to that) but whether he himself, the Boy, and Godot actually exist. In the series of questions he asks the Boy, he is more intent on getting himself a conversational partner to thwart the silence (Estragon has not spoken since he went off to nurse his foot) than in learning anything meaningful about the Boy's situation at home. That the Boy provides answers to fascinate symbol-hunting literary critics ('I mind the goats, Sir' his brother 'minds the sheep, Sir' and gets beaten) is part of the provocation of the scene. But Vladimir makes nothing of these answers and is concerned only with insuring that the Boy tell Godot 'you saw us'.

Esse est percipi ('to be is to be perceived') — Beckett often quotes the concept at the heart of Bishop Berkeley's philosophical thought, which is also central to his own fiction and drama. According to Berkeley, the universe exists only by virtue of God's continued perception of it. Vladimir's mounting dread at this moment in the play comes from his suspicion that if the Boy was not here yesterday and does not tell Godot that he saw the two men on the country road, then their very existences are rendered precarious.

Just at this moment – the most serious threat of deprivation in a play in which progressive loss is a governing principle – the Boy exits running, the light fails, the stagy moon suddenly rises at the back, and it is night once more. Larry Held, who played Estragon in the San Quentin Drama Workshop production, recalls Beckett saying that when the moon rises Vladimir and Estragon have nothing left, 'they're both exhausted, they're at the end'. Asked by the actors for advice about how to play this sequence, Beckett said: 'Speak with the tone of moonlight in your voices.'

The closing scene of Act I *does* have a blanched quality about it: the whiteness of a steady, progressive deprivation and disillusionment. But moonlight is only one hue (even if the governing one) in a wide spectrum of colours. Vladimir's opening 'At last!' seems a conclusive enough welcome to the coming of dark night, but Estragon's meticulous placing of his boots at the edge of the stage introduces a note of beginning again, of getting ready for a new day. What follows is similarly a blend of many different colours, sounds, rhythms, and moods that creates an atmosphere surprisingly magical as well as desolate. Estragon's answer 'Pale for weariness' to Vladimir's question 'What are you doing?' seems nonsensical unless one is familiar with the quotation from 'To the Moon', a lyric poem in which Shelley addresses the moon as being 'pale for weariness / Of climbing heaven and gazing on the earth, / Wandering companionless / Among the stars that have a different birth . . .' Certainly the image is chaste and forlorn, but it reminds us that Estragon is still the poet that he earlier claimed to be; and in this scene he and Vladimir alternate between confessing their hopelessness and finding a language to give despair a meaning that transcends desperation.

With comic generosity, Estragon wants to leave his boots behind for some passer-by with smaller feet, 'and they'll make him happy'.

VLADIMIR: But you can't go barefoot!
ESTRAGON: Christ did.
VLADIMIR: Christ! What's Christ got to do with it? You're not going to compare yourself to Christ!
ESTRAGON: All my life I've compared myself to him.
VLADIMIR: But where he lived it was warm, it was dry!
ESTRAGON: Yes. And they crucified quick.   (F, 52; G, 34+)

Ludicrous in its extravagant inapplicability, excessive in its self-pity, Estragon's claim is also plaintively fitting for the plight of an itinerant longing for a connection with the spiritual hero who embodied the promise of salvation for all mankind through his suffering and theirs.

More evidence of desperate kinship follows. After agreeing that they have 'nothing more to do here . . . or anywhere else', the two friends temporarily take heart again in the Boy's message that Godot is sure to come tomorrow; and Vladimir tries several times to lead Estragon tenderly by the arm and move towards shelter (the tableau that Beckett said *is* the play. Estragon, never without the imagination of disaster, talks about coming back tomorrow with 'a bit of rope'. Vladimir renews the nudging effort to draw him away, and Estragon suddenly recalls the time years ago when he tried to end it all by throwing himself into the Rhône:

VLADIMIR: We were grape-harvesting.
ESTRAGON: You fished me out.
VLADIMIR: That's all dead and buried.
ESTRAGON: My clothes dried in the sun.
VLADIMIR: There's no good harking back on that. Come on.
            He draws him after him. As before. (F, 53; G, 35)

An attempt at suicide under a warm sun in harvest season, a friend to the rescue, a need to remember and to forget, and a renewed effort at going on. A moment later, the unregenerate Estragon draws away and wonders aloud if 'we wouldn't have been better off alone, each one for himself'. And then, in perhaps the most plangently ironical line of the play, he concludes: 'We weren't made for the same road' — this from the man who now seems destined to spend eternity with his friend Vladimir, 'at this place, until the fall of night', waiting for Godot. And then the closing tableau that embodies

desire and stasis in one unforgettable image. Estragon crosses
the stage and sits on his mound; Vladimir slowly moves across
and sits down beside Estragon:

ESTRAGON: Well, shall we go?
VLADIMIR: Yes, let's go.
They do not move. (F, 54; G, 35 +)

Act I/Act II – 'nothing happens, twice'

Vivian Mercier's often quoted witticism that in *Waiting for
Godot* 'nothing happens, *twice*' gets at something essential in
the structure of Beckett's play. Nothing does happen, at least
twice, and on different levels: Godot fails to appear in each
act, denying the audience the expected consummation of a
traditional plot; and on two different days Vladimir and
Estragon experience shuddery perceptions of the vacancy of
their lives and respond with a series of seemingly pointless
routines in which 'nothing' is made magically to happen. But
despite surface similarities, the second act is strikingly different in texture, tone, and implication from the first, and it
provides a marked intensification and development of the
play's central subject: what people do to pass the time while
waiting.

Although Act II takes place at evening on the next day, the
events seem to be happening at a far more advanced stage in
the process of frustrated waiting and by implication in the
history of modern civilization. Everything still occurs in
circles and repetition continues to rule, but the recurrences
are asymmetrical (repetition with a difference) and within the
circle there has been a precipitous decline. In the opening
tableau, the boots and the hat appear to have seized centre
stage from the human beings; and in the first pantomime,
Vladimir scurrying back and forth seems even more perturbed
than he had been in Act I. The tree with its four or five new
leaves may be an emblem of hope, but more faint by far than
it was in the original French version where 'L'arbre est
couvert de feuilles'; and Beckett has insisted that the meagre
flowering was meant only to record the passage of time.

The comic song with which Vladimir opens the second act
parallels in a surprising way Lucky's bravura performance,
for it, too, gathers the threads and themes of the play
together. Its form is circular; its subject-matter is violence
and extinction; it embodies a bizarre resurrection within its
repeated stanzas; and the account of the dog made immortal
by having his story told and retold on a tombstone 'for the
eyes of dogs to come' is strangely consoling. And if that were
not enough, Vladimir is thrice said to stop, brood, and
resume.

Estragon is more frightened, gloomily pessimistic, quick to
fly into a rage and lash out at the scenery as well as at his
friend, who has been trying to put on a cheerful face and lift
their spirits. Although Gogo's irascibility makes it almost
impossible for any dialogue to be sustained for long, the main
hindrance to conversation is less Gogo's behaviour than the
fact that they've been through these exchanges so many times
before. The routines in the early minutes of Act II are
truncated because the material is overly familiar; it has in a
sense already been 'used up'. Because of the tedium and
impoverishment of their lives, autobiography as a source for
keeping the conversation going is running dry. The two men
have long known the answer to all the old questions: when
Vladimir asks 'Did they beat you?' he doesn't even bother to
wait for a reply. When he takes the new tack of trying to
speculate on why Estragon always comes back, he suggests
that it is because his friend doesn't know how to defend
himself; but the morose Gogo keeps insisting 'I wasn't doing
anything', a denial that elicits from Vladimir the reminder
that in this life, style is of the essence: 'It's the way of doing
it that counts, the way of doing it, if you want to go on living.'

It takes a while, though, for this important lesson to sink
in. The next few exchanges (about happiness, waiting for
Godot, the tree, the encounter yesterday with Pozzo and
Lucky, and living years ago in the Macon country) are short-
circuited because of the stale familiarity of the material. A
breakthrough occurs when Estragon decides finally to play
the game on Vladimir's terms:

ESTRAGON: In the meantime let us try and converse calmly, since we are incapable of keeping silent.

VLADIMIR: You're right, we're inexhaustible.

ESTRAGON: It's so we won't think.

VLADIMIR: We have that excuse.

ESTRAGON: It's so we won't hear.

VLADIMIR: We have our reasons.

ESTRAGON: All the dead voices.

VLADIMIR: They make a noise like wings.

ESTRAGON: Like leaves.

VLADIMIR: Like sand.

ESTRAGON: Like leaves.
Silence.

VLADIMIR: They all speak at once.

ESTRAGON: Each one to itself.
Silence.

VLADIMIR: Rather they whisper.

ESTRAGON: They rustle.

VLADIMIR: They murmur.

ESTRAGON: They rustle.
Silence.

VLADIMIR: What do they say?

ESTRAGON: They talk about their lives.

VLADIMIR: To have lived is not enough for them.

ESTRAGON: They have to talk about it.

VLADIMIR: To be dead is not enough for them.

ESTRAGON: It is not sufficient.
Silence.

VLADIMIR: They make a noise like feathers.

ESTRAGON: Like leaves.

VLADIMIR: Like ashes.

ESTRAGON: Like leaves.
Long silence.

VLADIMIR: Say something!

ESTRAGON: I'm trying.
Long silence.

VLADIMIR: (*in anguish*). Say anything at all!

ESTRAGON: What do we do now?

VLADIMIR: Wait for Godot.

ESTRAGON: Ah!
Silence.   (F, 62–3, G, 40–1)

On the page and in the theatre this hauntingly beautiful set-piece is recognizably more poetic and musical than any of the routines that have occurred in the play until now. With a structure scarcely distinguishable from densely figurative, patterned free verse, the dialogue moves forward in chiselled lines that regularly vary two, three, four, and five beats. Repetition, measured refrains, alliteration, and assonance are notably marked; and − given the eerie subject of the passage − it is useful to recall John Hollander's reminder that 'Assonance is the spirit of a rhyme, /A common vowel, hovering like a sigh / After its consonantal body dies.' But it is not only the economical, strongly cadenced language that makes the passage seem so exquisitely self-conscious. The two friends themselves are slyly complicitous, much like intimates sharing special knowledge and secrets. Attuned so well to each other's deepest thoughts, deftly providing lines to quicken a lyrical movement, they are likely to make us feel almost as if we are intruding on their privacy.

The secret they seem to be sharing expands our sense not only of their dilemma but of their capacity for dealing with it as well. Different from all the routines up to this point, the litany of the dead voices is an imaginative leap into the dark, an attempt to pass the time by extending the boundaries of the physical world to animate figures who have no material substance, and to envision predicaments that seem (at least in the beginning) to be beyond any that Didi and Gogo themselves can have experienced.

By creating a contrapuntal exchange in which the dead are perceived as phantom voices obliged to speak of their lives in the most shiveringly modulated of tones, Vladimir and Estragon go far beyond their talk about boots and hats, carrots and turnips, the prospect of meeting Godot, of understanding the Gospels, or of committing suicide. At first, the imagined scene seems like an act of sympathetic generosity − an effort to provide for the ghosts their own liturgical music. But when we probe the sense of the sound, it becomes clear that something more elaborate is going on. Although the two friends gain some solace and release by entering the world of apparitions they themselves create, they are also recognizing their mournful kinship with those who no longer exist.

Death, in a macabre turn, is seen to be actually no better

than life: the dead, like Didi and Gogo, are inexplicably obliged to speak on in pursuit of some finality, some promised end that seems permanently beyond them. In the perception that nothing is sufficient, not even death, there is terror but also a characteristically Beckettian consolation. As the Unnamable puts it: 'The essential is never to arrive anywhere, never to be anywhere, neither where Mahood is, nor where Worm is, nor where I am . . . The essential is to go on squirming forever at the end of the line.'

If death is not sufficient, language is hardly going to be able to provide closure or permanence. As the two friends intone the lives of the dead, their own words run down: a chant that began with leaves/sand/leaves closes with leaves/ashes/leaves, two *long silences*, and Vladimir's anguished 'Say anything at all!' As Hugh Kenner has pointed out, the climactic ritual exchange about waiting for Godot that follows 'has its ritual termination like an Amen, the shortest utterance in the play, the monosyllable 'Ah!' (*Reader's Guide*, pp. 34–5).

From this point on, the intricately orchestrated routines in the middle of the second act encompass and go beyond those that occurred in the first, gaining from the self-awareness of the couple an increased urgency and a heightened sense of need. Much of the inspired zaniness is still there, but the two friends are more apt now to admit that they are desperately playing roles, and these admissions spur them to greater inventiveness, at the same time that they reveal their keen sense of the insufficiency of their resources, the limits of their resiliency. Most of the earlier routines had been provoked by some concrete aspect of their situation – a tight boot, a lice-infested hat, the specifics of their appointment with Godot, or the immediate question of whether they should hang themselves. Now the routines in the middle of Act II are provoked mainly by a more general realization that to pass the time and ward off the silence, talk must be sustained for its own sake, and this late in the day, conversation means invention.

What follows, then, are dialogues fuelled by panic but

more openly designed by the role-playing participants than many of those that came before. Estragon coolly says 'Let's ask each other questions' or 'Let's contradict each other' (where earlier he was likely to say 'Let's hang ourselves'). These more knowingly deliberate exchanges are full of shrewd observations about method, process, style, and theatre itself; and they incorporate their own tart self-criticism: 'This is awful!' or 'This is becoming really insignificant.' Estragon emerges as more of a philosopher than he had been previously, observing that no matter where they wait for Godot 'there's no lack of void'. And it is Estragon who provides the handsome compliment to himself and his friend at the end of the nimble yet sinister routine about thinking: 'That wasn't such a bad little canter.' The word 'canter' is the perfect choice here, not only because 'an easy gallop' is so exact a description for the graceful pace of the unnerving dialogue, but because the word is short for Canterbury and means to ride at an easy pace like that of Chaucer's pilgrims, who also famously told stories to help pass the time on a road.

But no matter how crafty they are, Vladimir and Estragon run out of words and images for their imaginative efforts to keep the discourse going, and they have to turn back to the old stand-bys, Gogo's boots and Didi's radishes and turnips. The boots, though, haven't lost their magic, and it is just after the friends agree that Gogo's putting them back on would be something of 'a relaxation', 'a recreation', that he makes his most telling and unforgettable philosophical observation: 'We don't manage too badly, eh Didi, between the two of us? . . . We always find something, eh Didi, to give us the impression we exist?' (F, 69; G, 44 +). As Vladimir grudgingly agrees, he and his friend are magicians, and − in the enclosed world of their invented routines − they are also surprising surrogates for Berkeley's God, guaranteeing the existence of the universe and its inhabitants by perceiving it. But they are also in a curious way precursors of late twentieth-century post modernist artists: mindful of absurdity, the burden of self-consciousness, and the insufficiency of their own means of expression. And they are post-modern, too, in their commitment to the belief that life itself is indistinguishable from theatre and that to say is to invent, to create enabling fictions.

The most notable example of this comes just after Didi and Gogo perform the delectable juggling routine in which three hats rotate on two heads (inspired by the scene between Chico, Harpo and the lemonade vendor in the Marx Brothers' *Duck Soup*); and Estragon then announces 'I'm going.' Vladimir's proposal that they now try to pass the time playing Pozzo and Lucky ends in a fiasco because Gogo's memory is disintegrating and Didi himself cannot 'think' like Lucky. Pozzo turns out to have been too histrionic and Lucky too frighteningly genuine for them to be successfully imitated here. From this point, the frantic tempo quickens, the already well-developed sense of panic intensifies, and the action becomes increasingly grotesque. The climactic moment is Gogo's alarming report that 'They're coming!' Vladimir, exhausted and needful, shouts triumphantly that 'It's Godot! At last! Gogo! It's Godot! We're saved!' and he tries once more (in the play's emblematic gesture) to draw Estragon towards the wings. After their confused, futile effort to flee the bounds of the theatre, the two men decide to keep their own highly distinctive vigil to wait for Godot (a vigil that will strike any audience as the most ludicrous and at the same time perhaps the most appealingly winning of defences). Temporarily, their powers of invention are rekindled: they perform an ingenious cursing match (abusing themselves in the absence of the Saviour the two thieves had abused); they touchingly make up and embrace, do their end-of-day exercises, and at Vladimir's suggestion attempt to imitate the tree.

VLADIMIR: . . . Let's just do the tree, for the balance.
ESTRAGON: The tree?
            Vladimir does the tree, staggering about on one leg.
VLADIMIR: (*stopping*). Your turn.
            Estragon does the tree, staggers.
ESTRAGON: Do you think God sees me?
VLADIMIR: You must close your eyes.
            Estragon closes his eyes, staggers worse.
ESTRAGON: (*stopping, brandishing his fists, at the top of his voice.*) God have pity on me!

VLADIMIR: (*vexed*). And me?
ESTRAGON: On me! On me! Pity! On me!   (F, 76–7; G, 49)

In several respects, this is one of the most suggestive of all Vladimir and Estragon's routines, for it expresses in a brilliant cameo so many of the associations that have been accruing throughout the play. For many audiences, the spare tree alone on stage is likely to suggest different trees in mythical literature that symbolize hope, divine life, and immortality. For some, it is likely to be reminiscent of the cross, and it might also echo the allusion in Act I to the tree of life mentioned in the Book of Proverbs (although it has been associated by some with the tree on which Judas hanged himself). Others have connected it to Dante's tree at the gate of hell, to the Buddhist Bo tree, to Pascal's 'thinking reed', and to Yggdrasil, the tree that spread over the world in Norse mythology. In notable performances of *Godot*, designers have taken pains to create unrealistic assemblages that have subterranean force. The original production featured a tree of brown crêpe paper wound around coathangers mounted on a foam rubber base. For the Schiller Theater in Berlin, the designer Matias created a curved semi-abstraction to relate to the circles, arcs, and diagonals of Beckett's geometric configuration. Most famously, in Paris in 1961, the sculptor Giacometti moulded plaster on thin branching wire to suggest the reach and fragility of hope. During the rehearsals, he and Beckett would sit for hours trying to get the tree to fulfil an elusive ideal of slenderness. 'It never seemed right', Giacometti recalled, 'and each of us said to the other: maybe' (Lord, p. 429). A decade later, Beckett was heard to remark: 'How sad . . . the tree was destroyed. The tree at the Odéon was destroyed in sixty-eight. Giacometti's tree . . . The Godot tree' (Calder, p. 103). But Alan Schneider once wrote that Beckett did not intend Didi's exercise to be at all a representation of the tree on stage, but rather one of the basic positions of yoga 'in which the sole of one foot is placed directly alongside the calf of the other, with the two hands clasped together as if in prayer' (Morot-Sir, p. 280).

As Ruby Cohn has wittily observed, it is no small wonder

that Vladimir and Estragon stagger when they 'do' the tree. Yet 'doing the tree' is one of the most telling of Beckett's mimes, not only because of symbolic reverberations, but because the scene expresses so much of what has been happening up till now in the dramatic movement of the entire play. Here, Didi and Gogo again find a consummate style for their despair, blending all of their characteristic tones. Vladimir's suggestion that they do the tree 'for the balance' reveals something of the speculative man's desire to move the earlier set of mundane exercises to some loftier level of poise and harmony. Estragon's puzzled reply 'The tree?' may look at first like dimwittedness, but he is being quite sensible in wondering what else he and his friend might be able to do with the tree other than hang themselves from it. The sight of the seedy old men, each trying in turn to perch nimbly on one leg and then staggering about like the clowns they so frequently resemble, is acrid comedy: the body in Beckett is always the mind's subversive partner, laughably undermining its dreamy attempts to create order. Estragon's query about whether God sees him is startling, partly because it can be read as evidence that Godot must be a person, but equally importantly, because it displays a fervent spirituality (as well as deep fright) that we haven't seen in Gogo before. Vladimir understands the need for humility in the eyes of God, but when Estragon closes *his* eyes, he totters even more, a poignant revelation of the solitude and egotism that are reinforced a moment later when he excludes Vladimir from his prayer for God's pity. Through the discomforting humour, the urgency of the prayer comes across as heartfelt, and Estragon's exclusion of his friend is proof of just how terrified he actually is. But the religious implications of 'doing the tree' are quickly nullified, or at least rendered ironical, by the entrance of Pozzo and Lucky.

Pozzo *redux*

When Pozzo arrived on the scene in Act I, he was a power to be reckoned with: if not Godot, then Lord of the Manor, brutalizing his slave and intimidating the derelicts looking on astonished. Crossing back now he is a figure in flight: blind, led by Lucky on a shorter rope, and collapsing in noisy disorder to the ground. Pozzo's 'fall' is the governing image of the middle part of Act II, defining the conditions under which the next phase of waiting will take place. Although things have been running down steadily since Vladimir sang his round about the dog, the cook and the tombstone, the action here is moving into an even more advanced stage of degeneration. The signs of accelerating confusion are many. There is more exaggeration and broad farce in the second sequence with Pozzo and Lucky than anywhere else in the play — more laughable misidentifications and absurdity — indeed, a sense that travesty now rules this world. People are more cruel than ever before. The self-absorbed Vladimir pontificates windily while Pozzo lies crying for help; Estragon suggests that they exploit the prostrate master for money; and he then kicks and curses Lucky with a fury so concentrated that it makes Pozzo's earlier behaviour seem almost gentle. In the first act Didi and Gogo felt compassion for Lucky, here (in the tradition of the two thieves) they abuse him.

Most of the ludicrous reunion scene takes place after all four men have progressively dropped to the ground, a slow-motion descent that Beckett sees as 'the visual expression of their common situation', related to 'the threat of everything in the play falling' (Fletcher, *Student's Guide*, pp. 72–3). The scene has all the momentum and drollery of a star tumbling-act at a clown show, but it has a sober, insinuating side as well, and as a stage in the process of disintegration it provokes uneasiness. The figures on the ground keep making and dissolving cruciform patterns, a choreography that is sometimes described as 'empty crosses', implying — among other things — the inadequacy of Pozzo as saviour, but also the way in which these absurd sufferers are linked to an emblem of suffering that has meaning and coherence.

Revealing, too, about this world in decline is the extreme mix of moments when the characters are laughably self-deceived and others when they are delightfully sly and insightful. Generally, Vladimir and Estragon are as addle-

brained here as at any point in the play. They miss simple con-
nections, fail to notice for the longest time that Pozzo is
blind, and are continually caught up in ridiculous antics that
have little to do with what is actually happening in front of
them. But it is on 'sweet mother earth' with Pozzo and Lucky
that they play one of their wiliest games (conjuring up Cain
and Abel), and it is here, too, that they surprise us with their
amusingly exact use of a classical learning we never suspected
they had. Tired of propping Pozzo up, Estragon observes that
'we are not caryatids' (sculptured female figures used as col-
umns); while Vladimir provides the Latin tag to support his
contention that the blind Pozzo must be thinking of the days
when he was happy ('*Memoria praeteritorum bonorum*'). It
is here, too, that Estragon admits that he understands what
he is doing on this God-forsaken country road:

POZZO: What is he waiting for?
VLADIMIR: What are you waiting for?
ESTRAGON: I'm waiting for Godot.

Not only is this the first time that Gogo admits straight out
that he is waiting for Godot, but it is the first time that either
man uses 'I' rather than 'We', which is more evidence of
diminishing fraternity in their world.

  The other startling moment when a character emerges from
the absurdity of broad farce to talk in a way that strikes
through the mask of customary or clownish rhetoric comes
when Pozzo responds in fury to Vladimir's badgering about
how long Lucky has been dumb:

Have you not done tormenting me with your accursed time! It's
abominable! When! When! One day, is that not enough for you, one
day like any other day, one day he went dumb, one day I went blind,
one day we'll go deaf, one day we were born, one day we shall die,
the same day, the same second, is that not enough for you?
(*Calmer.*) They give birth astride of a grave, the light gleams an instant, then it's night once more. (*He jerks the rope.*) On!

(F, 89; G, 57 +)

Although this diatribe has Pozzo's recognizable melo-
dramatic swagger, it comes across with the fiery authenticity
of the last words of the stricken hero in a Greek or

Shakespearean tragedy. How does such an extraordinary transformation take place? How does Beckett achieve such resonance and persuasiveness from the epitome of stagy ostentation at the close of a sequence that has been so outlandishly farcical and grotesque? To understand this is to move towards an explanation of another essential aspect of Beckett's dramatic art.

In one respect, Pozzo's vehement summation is like Lucky's: it appears to come out of the blue and yet is connected in innumerable ways to all the major themes of the play. From the start of *Waiting for Godot*, Vladimir and Estragon have been obsessively talking about the problems posed by time: how to pass it or bide it; what they did with it yesterday or long ago in the Macon country; what they should have done with it 'a million years ago, in the nineties'; how it will surely be better tomorrow when Godot comes. Even the master and his man have their strong opinions about time. Pozzo knows what the local twilights can do before night bursts upon us 'on this bitch of an earth'; and Lucky wants to believe in a personal God with a white beard 'outside time without extension', but has ultimately to admit that 'for reasons unknown time will tell . . . time will tell'.

Part of the force of Pozzo's speech comes from the ancient belief that blind men are invested with prophetic powers and declaim universal truths, so when he lashes out at Didi and Gogo's reflexive way of dealing with the problem of time, his assault carries extraordinary weight. From Pozzo's darkness, the span of a human life doesn't stretch in interludes to be filled by habit and invention, but passes in a terrifying flash: the midwife and the grave-digger appear on the scene simultaneously. Expressed in terse, propulsive, dazzlingly original language, at a point in the play when we have been watching demonstrations of endless ingenuity in the passing of time, Pozzo's paradoxical lament that there isn't any time to pass is likely to strike most audiences as being chillingly indisputable.

But just as Vladimir and Estragon paid no attention to Lucky when he told them about God, Man and Nature in Act I, they ignore Pozzo on Time now. Yet the differences in their

disregard reveal how far they have travelled between yesterday and today. After Pozzo's 'On! Adieu! Pig! Yip! Adieu!'
in the first act, the diverted Vladimir said, 'That passed the
time', and when Estragon observed that it would have passed
in any case, he replied 'Yes, but not so rapidly.' Now, Pozzo's
'On!' is heard only by Vladimir, since Estragon is fast asleep,
and when Didi shakes him awake, the exchange shows an
even greater intensification of uncertainty and anguish.
Estragon comes back into consciousness with wild gestures
and incoherent words, complains that his friend never lets
him sleep, and announces: 'I was dreaming I was happy.'
Vladimir's reply: 'That passed the time' could now refer
either to Gogo's announcement or the interlude with Pozzo
and Lucky. In either event, the subsequent talk about whether
or not Pozzo was really blind is based on Vladimir's continued need to be perceived ('It seemed to me he saw us').
Estragon's rejoinder 'You dreamt it. (*Pause.*) Let's go. We
can't. Ah!' completes the cycle begun a few minutes before
when he admitted that he was waiting for Godot. By now, as
this compacted sentence suggests, Estragon has for the first
time got the whole picture clear in his mind at once; but his
subsequent response is to fog things up all over again:

ESTRAGON: Are you sure it wasn't him?
VLADIMIR: Who?
ESTRAGON: Godot.
VLADIMIR: But who?
ESTRAGON: Pozzo.
VLADIMIR: Not at all! (*Less sure.*) Not at all! (*Still less sure.*) Not
　　　　　at all!　　　　　　　　　　　　　　(F, 90; G, 58)

Moments later Vladimir delivers his great soliloquy and the
play moves towards its ending.

Vladimir's soliloquy, the Boy again, the close of the play

Vladimir's soliloquy comes at a pivotal moment in the action
of the play. Pozzo and Lucky have just left; Estragon has
demonstrated his clearest understanding of what he and his
friend are doing at this forsaken spot and why they can't

leave. He sits down, tries to take off his boot, calls out 'Help me!' and gets in response Vladimir's ardent and intimate reflections on the meaning of his life. In one sense, the speech follows the ironical, deflationary pattern of many others before it: someone calls for help, someone else offers solemn ponderings on his own predicament, and there is no evidence that the words are being heard. But in every other respect, Vladimir's soliloquy is like the tirades of Lucky and Pozzo and the dialogue of the dead voices: an astonishing move into a previously uncharted territory, a genuine attempt at truth-telling fit for a drama of unknowingness.

By beginning with six speculative questions, Vladimir seems to be trying to get beyond the realm of habit and routine, to achieve some kind of heightened understanding of what has really been happening to him and what it means. But the effort puts him further than ever into a perceptual limbo where distinctions between appearance and reality, today and tomorrow have dissolved. His opening query about whether he was asleep in the past and is perhaps sleeping now is so radical that it confirms the dreamscape as the governing reality of his life, as it has been of the play. Like Shakespeare's Prospero (but without his magic and command), Vladimir sees that he is 'such stuff as dreams are made on' and his little life 'is rounded with a sleep'.

If this is his true condition, then what meaning can there be to his having waited with his friend at this place until the fall of night for someone named Godot? As he ponders this, Vladimir glances at the dozing Estragon and reconstructs one of their customary exchanges: 'He'll know nothing. He'll tell me about the blows he received and I'll give him a carrot', a melancholy affirmation of friendship as one of the enduring positive values of the play. But the echo of Pozzo's fiery assault on time is still in the air and Vladimir, accepting the grim premise, offers his own very personal version of Pozzo's text:

Astride of a grave and a difficult birth. Down in the hole, lingeringly, the grave-digger puts on the forceps. We have time to grow old. The air is full of our cries. (*He listens.*) But habit is a great deadener. (*He looks again at Estragon.*) At me too someone is looking, of me too someone is saying, he is sleeping, he knows nothing,

let him sleep on. (*Pause*.) I can't go on! (*Pause*.) What have I said?
(F, 90; G, 58)

For Pozzo birth and death are condensed into a single second; for Vladimir birth is difficult and the grave-digger works slowly, leaving us just enough time to feel and know and respond to human suffering in a world without meaning and purpose. But this tormented perception, so starkly yet magnificently expressed, is itself subject to terrifying question. If, as Vladimir surmises, there is someone perceiving him, perhaps judging his despair to be dreamy ignorance and deciding to leave him to it, then he is more abandoned than he ever knew. It is this awful revelation − that there may be a force judging him for an inability to imagine his way out of his own nihilistic despair − that leads Vladimir to utter for the first time the most desolate of all words in the Beckett world: 'I can't go on'.

Much of the evocative power of Vladimir's soliloquy comes from its being so confessional and unaffected, an anguished utterance that has little to do with role-playing or stylish routines to pass the time. At this moment of genuinely bitter negation, Godot's emissary comes, with all ironies intact, as a kind of *deus ex machina*, leading Vladimir back into a world in which meaning must always be reconstituted and which at the same time is deadened by habit. Having asked the questions before and knowing the answers in advance, Vladimir puts the boy through an abbreviated drill that has only two new but vital questions: What does Mr Godot do and does he have a beard? Both answers ('He does nothing, Sir' and 'I think it's white, Sir') link Godot by punning and other verbal correspondences back to just about everybody and everything else in the play. But the second answer has an effect that carries forward. Vladimir's exclamation, 'Christ have mercy on us!' is the first of several of his expressions phrased in an unequivocal religious vocabulary of punishment, mercy, and salvation. At this moment of his fright and solitude, Vladimir (like some members of Beckett's audience) seems to be imagining Godot as God, for to paraphrase an observation of Jean-Jacques Mayoux, God here 'is a fable invented by man in his state of abandonment, a projection of himself, a reflection of all the things that seem on the human plane to reflect' Him (Esslin, *Samuel Beckett*, p. 78). But Vladimir resists the equation between Godot and God, as the play does.

The closing scene is often cited as one of the supreme instances of the richness of Beckett's theatrical poetry, for it blends stunning visual and aural effects to achieve a perfect synthesis of metaphysical desperation and meticulously performed slapstick comedy. After the Boy exits running, the mechanical moon rises, bathing in pale light the two men sunk in futility. Vladimir stands motionless and bowed, as if he is performing some ritual expressing at once his heightened awareness of despair and his frightened relapse into habit. In another gesture of respect, the awakening Estragon removes his boots and places them centre front, carefully ordering the little in his world susceptible to order. The dialogue could hardly be more stripped or disconsolate, or witty. ('What's wrong with you?' Estragon asks. 'Nothing', says Vladimir with bitter accuracy.) Estragon then weakly takes the physical initiative for the first time in the play, drawing Vladimir towards the tree where now they both stand motionless (a sad reminder of the other moments when Didi led him towards the wings). Like so much else in the second act, the following discussion of suicide is at a more advanced stage of completion than it had been in Act I. There Estragon had asked to be reminded to bring a bit of rope tomorrow. Here he proposes straight out that they hang themselves, offering his worn belt as a substitute for the rope they do not have, and he finds Vladimir agreeable enough. When Estragon takes off the belt and his pants drop to his ankles, the farcical vignette is fraught with tension. The dropping of a clown's pants is one of the oldest and most effective of circus and music-hall jokes – the ultimate assault on male dignity and a rib-tickling sign of powerlessness and dependency. But that is only half of the visual sequence. When the two men test the potency of their suicide instrument and the belt breaks, they nearly fall to the ground, illustrating in their comic stagger the hopelessness not only of their lives but of all their efforts to end them. And yet the next sequence illustrates the brilliant orchestration of hope and hopelessness that is one of the most affecting rhythms of the play.

ESTRAGON: You say we have to come back tomorrow?
VLADIMIR: Yes.
ESTRAGON: Then we can bring a good bit of rope.
VLADIMIR: Yes.

But again not for long:

ESTRAGON: Didi.
VLADIMIR: Yes.
ESTRAGON: I can't go on like this.

But again:

VLADIMIR: That's what you think.

But comically the perseverance seems good for only twenty-four hours, and yet the old dream of a last-minute rescue is built into the desperation.

VLADIMIR: We'll hang ourselves tomorrow. (*Pause.*) Unless Godot comes.
ESTRAGON: And if he comes?
VLADIMIR: We'll be saved.   (F, 94; G, 60)

At the end of Act I, both men were sitting, facing the audience from the mound; here they are standing next to the tree they associate with life and death. Earlier, Estragon began the closing routine with 'Well, shall we go?' Now he begins with 'Well? Shall we go?' – a second question mark and a soft break replacing the earlier comma and a hard one, intensifying the renewed note of eroded certainty and of despair. The exchange about the trousers sounds like an outlandish protracting of the hoary vaudeville gag, but it gets new life here not only from the context but from Estragon's buffoonish twisting of the question, which allows Vladimir to repeat emphatically Lucky's word, Pozzo's word and Beckett's, 'Pull ON your trousers'. Now it is Vladimir's turn for elegant variation, as he asks 'Well? Shall we go?' and Estragon's 'Yes, let's go', is the line Vladimir uttered at the end of Act I. In the frozen moment of stasis that closes the play, the friends have never seemed so nakedly exposed, so ruefully comic and, in their beleaguered hopefulness, so constant.

Chapter 3

Godot in French and in English

It is very rare in world literature for a landmark to exist in two languages both of which are the author's own. Because the French original and the English translation of *Godot* are Beckett's creations, it is inevitable that we should want to compare the two versions and to generalize about their differences. As we have already seen, *En attendant Godot* was written between 9 October 1948 and 29 January 1949, published on 17 October 1952, and first performed on 5 January 1953. The stir caused by the play quickly brought Beckett hundreds of inquiries and proposals about *Godot* and his other work, and the months after the première were intensely busy. He was negotiating with the editors of the literary magazine, *Merlin*, and with Maurice Girodias of Olympia Press for the publication of *Watt* (printed in August), conferring with Patrick Bowles and Richard Seaver about the translations of *Molloy* and 'La Fin', discussing with Jerome Lindon preparations for the publication of *L'Innommable* (set for July), corresponding with Barney Rosset of Grove Press for the translation and publication of the novels and the play, and with theatre people around the world about performances of *Godot*. Beckett began his own translation early in 1953, worked on it through the summer and autumn and sent Rosset a final version just after the new year 1954.

His main goal was to prepare the best possible script for performance in English, and the most noticeable differences between the two versions are cuts and changes he made to enhance the theatricality of the play. *Godot*, of course, was the first of Beckett's plays to be staged, and he learned a great deal about what worked and what didn't work during rehearsals and early performances at the Théâtre de Babylone. The most important of the differences between the two versions is that the English is more trim and in technical terms more explicit. Excess words are removed and four substantial passages of dialogue are omitted. In the first of these, Pozzo goes on tiresomely in a fifty-line sequence about how to present a brief and clear account of the ritual by which he asks Lucky to dance, sing, or think. The other three excised passages, totalling sixty-four lines, are variations on who-hit-and-didn't-help-whom from the second-act sequence in which the four men fall. In each instance, nothing of consequence has been lost, and the play undoubtedly gains in tempo and concentration from the cuts of passages that were not only indicative of boredom but boring in themselves.

The English *Godot* also has more specific stage directions. Early on in French, 'Vladimir sort'; in English he exits 'hurriedly'; Estragon, who says 'J'ai faim' in the original, says 'I'm hungry' 'violently' in the translation. And on several other occasions directions such as 'timidly', 'with extra vehemence' are added to indicate the author's desired emphasis in English. In the now-famous cursing match of Act II, the list of insults is specified in English but was originally improvised in French. Sometimes, a change in the stage directions indicate Beckett's change of mind about the desired effect. The Boy, for example, enters 'timidly' in English but 'craintivement' (fearfully) in French.

Several of the other alterations are clearly designed to heighten a specific theatrical moment or to develop a particular local possibility for an effect available in English but not in French. During the vaudeville exchange about why Lucky doesn't put down his bags, the French Vladimir keeps mechanically repeating 'Vous voulez vous en débarrasser?' while in English (after having several times said 'You want to get rid of him?') he adds an effective note of comic exasperation of the fifth of six repeats: 'You waagerrim?' At the end of Act I, when the moon rises, Vladimir asks Estragon: 'Qu'est-ce que tu fais?' [What are you doing?] and his friend answers: 'Je fais comme toi, je regarde la blafarde' [Same as you. I'm looking at the pale moon.] In English, Beckett has

Estragon answer with a quote from Shelley's lyrical fragment
'To the Moon':

ESTRAGON: Pale for weariness.
VLADIMIR: Eh?
ESTRAGON: Of climbing heaven and gazing on the likes of us.

We are again reminded that Estragon was perhaps once a poet
and that he is capable at this moment in English of a disillusionment deeper than is evident in the French response.

A similar point can be made about one other complex
variation in the translation. When Vladimir in the original
tells Estragon to leave Pozzo alone ('Ne vois-tu pas qu'il est
en train de se rappeler son bonheur. *Memoria praeteritorum
bonorum* – ca doit être pénible'), Pozzo replies 'Oui, bien
bonne'. [Can't you see he's thinking of the days when he was
happy. Happy memories pass by – that must be unpleasant
. . . Yes, wonderful, wonderful.] Pozzo is repeating a remark
about how good his sight was when he had it. In English,
however, Beckett cuts Pozzo's repetition and gives the reply
line to Estragon, who says 'We wouldn't know', a remark
that reveals his unhappiness and his surprising knowledge of
Latin.

In a number of other cases, however, Beckett made changes
that are less easy to assess, mainly because they seem to affect
the way the play simultaneously invites and resists religious
and allegorical interpretations and are thus themselves open
to different interpretation. At one point in French, for
instance, Pozzo explains that he is taking Lucky 'au marché
de Saint-Sauveur, où je compte bien en tirer quelque chose'.
In English, the name of the fair – which so directly suggests
the possibility of salvation – is eliminated, and the line proposes a more secular transaction: 'I am bringing him to the
fair, where I hope to get a good price for him.' Beckett may
have cut 'Saint-Sauveur' because he did not have a suitable
English equivalent, but he may also have wished to eliminate
the invitation to read allegorically.

In several other instances Beckett's choices for an English
equivalent make the text more ambiguous. During the

ludicrous exchange in which Pozzo bathetically claims that his servant is torturing *him*, Estragon's scolding of Lucky first takes the form 'Le faire souffrir ainsi', whereas in English he says 'Crucify him like that!' Then, just after Lucky is silenced and falls, Pozzo orders Vladimir and Estragon to raise him up (in a grotesque parody of Christ taken down from the cross). The exchange in the original reads:

POZZO: Allez, allez, soulevez-le!
ESTRAGON: Moi j'en ai marre. [I'm fed up with it (or) It bores me still.]

In English, there is a sacrilegious jest:

POZZO: Come on, come on, raise him up.
ESTRAGON: To hell with him!

Clearly these changes invite us to think about Christ more directly in English than in French, but on the other hand the invitation is so blatant and mocking that one could fairly interpret it as dismissive, an attempt to banish allegory by making it seem so preposterous.

Another problematical case is the passage in which Vladimir asks Estragon if he has ever read the Bible:

ESTRAGON: La Bible . . . (Il réfléchit.) J'ai dû y jeter un coup d'oeil. [The Bible . . . I must have taken a look at it.]
VLADIMIR: (*étonné*). A l'école sans Dieu? [Surprised. At the school without God?]
ESTRAGON: Sais pas si elle était sans ou avec. [Don't know whether it was without or with.]
VLADIMIR: Tu dois confondre avec la Roquette. [You must be mixing it up with Roquette.]

This elaborate passage must have posed several problems for Beckett when he was translating into English. Vladimir's question may be natural in French (did Estragon read the Bible in a secular or religious school?), and the response has a bluff humour to it; but in English the exchange is a clumsy and not entirely clear piece of pointing. (It is revealing to be told by Colin Duckworth (pp. 92–3) that the religious association and play on words do not appear in the manuscript, where Vladimir asks 'A l'école libre? and Estragon replies 'Sais pas si elle était libre'.) The part of the conversation about mixing the school up with Roquette must have been excised because it cannot make much sense in English. 'La Roquette' was until 1900 a prison in Paris, but the reference here is most likely to 'La Petite Roquette', a borstal or correction school for boys. Thinking that the first English audiences would have enough to be baffled by in the early moments of *Godot*, Beckett is likely to have cut the exchange for this reason alone.

Three other revisions along these lines are also teasingly difficult to interpret and have attracted a good deal of comment. One has to do with Estragon's name, another with Godot's habitat, and the third with Pozzo's 'knook'.

During the conversation in which Pozzo asks Didi and Gogo to request him to sit down, he addresses Estragon: 'Comment vous appelez-vous?' and Estragon replies 'Catulle', a response that provokes laughter and also relates to his earlier assertion that he used to be a poet. 'Catullus' appears in the early Faber text but is changed in the Grove Press edition to 'Adam'. Asked why he revised the name, Beckett explained 'We got fed up with Catullus', a reply that led Colin Duckworth to observe sensibly that if this were the only reason, 'one could justifiably take the author of *Waiting for Godot* to task for indulging in deliberate mystification. Why not choose a name like 'Bill' or 'Jones' which would conform more with Beckett's avowed principle of 'no symbols where none intended' (Duckworth, p. lxiv). But it is possible to explain the switch to Adam not as mystification but as deliberately blatant irony, a choice so exaggeratedly tendentious as to be comically meaningless and thus to rule out any symbolic interpretation at all.

The second revision − an omission − is similarly hard to assess. Early in Act I of the French original, when Vladimir and Estragon hear a noise and think it is Godot, there is another short exchange that Beckett eliminated in English.

ESTRAGON: Allons-nous-en. [Let's go.]
VLADIMIR: Où? (*Un temps.*) Ce soir on couchera peut-être chez

>   lui, au chaud, au sec, le ventre plein, sur la paille. Ça
>   vaut la peine qu'on attende. Non? [Where? Perhaps
>   tonight we will be sleeping at his place, warm, dry,
>   with full bellies on the straw. That's worth waiting
>   for, isn't it?]
>
> ESTRAGON: Pas toute la nuit. [Not all night.]
> VLADIMIR: Il fait encore jour. [It's still day.]

One can only speculate about Beckett's motives for eliminating this appealing passage, but he may have felt that the homely specificity of the details would establish too concrete a connection between the derelicts and Mr Godot, a connection that at this point in the play would best be left more mysterious (or to use a phrasing he prefers: 'vaguened'). Something similar occurs in another change that has nothing to do with translation as such. In the earliest version of the play, when Vladimir is confused about the day of the appointment with Godot, he fumbles about for a note on which Godot specified the date. No such note appears in the final French or English versions, an omission clearly designed to make the figure of Godot more shadowy and less substantial.

The third interesting change is in Pozzo's description of how, when he realized that beauty, grace, and truth were beyond him, he 'took a knook'. The word 'knook' seems to have been coined by Beckett by analogy with 'knut', Russian for 'whip'. In English, Vladimir asks for a definition of 'knook' but Pozzo ignores him. The French original has a longer passage on the subject that is omitted in English:

> VLADIMIR: Qu'est-ce que c'est, un knouk? [What's a knouk?]
> POZZO: Vous n'êtes pas d'ici. Etes-vous seulement du siècle?
>   Autrefois on avait des bouffons. Maintenant on a des
>   knouks. Ceux qui peuvent se le permettre. [You are
>   not from these parts. Are you so out of touch with the
>   times? Years ago people used to have jesters. Now they
>   have knouks. Those who are able to afford them.]

Although this passage is obscure in context, it can be taken to mean that Pozzo is claiming to have turned authoritarian when he realized that beauty, grace, and truth were beyond him – a stagy and unverifiable assertion. Again, it is not clear why Beckett would let Pozzo's explanation stand in French but not in English. A simple aesthetic explanation might suffice. The passage is neither dramatic nor revelatory and slows the action.

Among other matters that have stimulated a great deal of interest and have provoked disagreement are more general comparisons between the two versions. Is Beckett more colloquial in one language than in the other? Funnier? More philosophical? More vulgar? Lighter or darker? More elusive? In the twelfth chapter of her valuable early study, *Samuel Beckett: The Comic Gamut*, Ruby Cohn argues that the French *Godot* is more authentically colloquial and thereby more comic than the English rendering, which seems in her reading the bleaker of the two. More recently, in *From Desire to Godot*, she has pointed out that the play's opening word 'nothing' occurs more often later in that play than the French 'rien' and that Estragon's neutral repetitions of 'c'est vrai' become despairing 'ah's' in English. But in his perceptive essay 'Bilingual Playwright', Harry Cockerham argues that systematic comparison between the French and the English versions 'casts doubt on the notion that Beckett is more consistently poetic, or comic, or crude, or economical, or less enigmatic', in one language than the other (Worth, pp. 151–2).

A close look at the two versions tends to support Ruby Cohn on the questions of colloquialism and bleakness, but also reinforces Cockerham's argument about Beckett not being more consistently poetic or crude or enigmatic in one language than the other. At many places, the French version *is* more colloquial and informal than the English; there is more slang, Vladimir and Estragon's lofty moments are less lofty, and the whole tone is more generally down-and-out, though mostly in a comical way. Estragon is likely to say 'Tu m'as fait peur' [you scared me] in one language, but is more formal in the other: 'You gave me a fright.' If the English Pozzo rather elegantly observes that 'the fresh air stimulates the jaded appetite', his French counterpart says 'Le grand air, ça creuse', a more informal rendering [puts a hollow in my stomach]. Vivian Mercier recalls an amusing exchange in which he told Beckett that his translation of 'Ce serait un moyen de bander' (which the playwright had rendered 'It'd give us an erection') struck him as odd. Mercier said that the formality of the English made it sound as if Didi and Gogo had both got a Ph.D. Beckett slyly asked: 'How do you know they hadn't?' But Mercier stuck to his point that a true English equivalent for the slangy *bander* would have been 'It'd give us a hard-on' or as Joyce might have written, 'It'd make your micky stand for you' (*Beckett/Beckett*, p. 46).

Similarly, the English *Godot* does seem at times more bleak. There are of course the 'four or five leaves' on the tree in English, whereas in the French 'L'arbre est couvert de feuilles.' The English text is subtitled 'a tragicomedy in two acts', whereas the French is merely called 'pièce en deux actes', but tragicomedy can obviously go either way. The word 'nothing' does appear more often and in more philosophical ways than 'rien'. 'C'est vrai' is in context a less despairing, less vague, more affirmative response than 'ah!', for it suggests that the French Estragon has an understanding of what is going on and can agree with it, now that it has been called to his attention for the millionth time. It is interesting, though, to note again that in recent productions with which Beckett has been associated, the English Estragon says 'Ah, yes', which brings the phrase a good deal closer to the French. At times, rather small differences contribute to the feeling that the English version is more stripped down and grave. This exchange about the carrot is not unrepresentative:

VLADIMIR: Elle est bonne, ta carotte?
ESTRAGON: Elle est sucrée . . . Délicieuse, ta carotte.

VLADIMIR: How's the carrot?
ESTRAGON: It's a carrot . . . I'll never forget this carrot.

The French is more sensuous and positive; the English — where the carrot is a carrot and nothing more — is dryer and more ironic. Also, Estragon and Vladimir seem more panicked in English than in French. 'Alors comment faire?' [so what should we do] in the original becomes 'What'll we do, what'll we do!' in the translation.

On the question of which version is the more vulgar and

coarse-grained, there is supporting evidence on both sides of the case. At first glance, it looks as if the original might gain the nod for vulgarity. Estragon's early response to Vladimir's assertion about most people believing the Evangelist who reported that one of the thieves was saved is 'Les gens sont des cons' in one language and 'People are bloody ignorant apes' in the other − crude in both cases but a shade less so in current-day English. Later, when Estragon is bent over Pozzo's stomach trying to hear his watch and picks up his heartbeat instead, Pozzo in English disappointedly cries out 'damnation', whereas in French he shouts 'Merde alors!' In Act II, Vladimir has reservations about helping the fallen Pozzo get up, just in case the action should trigger violence from Lucky. In French the line reads: 'Que Lucky ne se mette en branle tout d'un coup. Alors nous serions baisés', whereas in English it is again less crude: 'That Lucky might get going all of a sudden. Then we'd be ballocksed.' But there are some notable exceptions. In the early exchange about Pozzo's name, Vladimir says 'J'ai connu une famille Gozzo. La mère brodait au tambour' [the mother did embroidery]. In English this becomes famously: 'The mother had the clap.' In French, Vladimir's response to eating is 'Je me fais au goût au fur et à mesure [I get used to the taste little by little]; in English: 'I get used to the muck as I go along.' In Act II, when Vladimir complains of 'this bastard Pozzo at it again', Estragon suggests that they 'Kick him in the crotch'. In the original, he proposes that they 'casse-lui la gueule' [kick his teeth in].

A brief review, then, of the differences between the French and English versions of *Godot* comes to an undramatic conclusion. Beckett clearly wrote the same work in English that he had originally composed in French, but he tried to make the second *Godot* more stageworthy and came to prefer the English for the performance text (which is often trimmed even further in rehearsals). When Beckett sat down to translate, he seems not to have been thinking in terms of tonal or thematic overviews: he did not set out to make the English *Godot* more of one thing than another (except more actable).

He worked word by word, line by line, trying to establish the most accurate and effective theatrical text possible. If *Godot* seems at times more colloquial and bleak in English than in French, the shadings are slight, and in nearly all other important respects the two versions are very similar. Most people who encounter *Godot* in French or in English experience essentially the same play.

Chapter 4

The presence of *Godot*: the play in the contemporary theatre and elsewhere

At the time when *Godot* was first done, it liberated something for anybody writing plays. It redefined the minima of theatrical validity. It was as simple as that. He got away. He won by twenty-eight lengths, and he'd done it with so little — and I mean that as an enormous compliment. There we all were, busting a gut with great monologues and pyrotechnics, and this extraordinary genius just put this play together with enormous refinement, and then with two completely unprecedented and uncategorisable bursts of architecture in the middle — terrible metaphor — and there it was, theatre.

(*The New Review*, Vol. 1, no. 9, December 1974, pp. 18–19)

The growing myth of *Godot*

The enthusiasm that Tom Stoppard expresses here in a 1974 talk with Ronald Hayman is symptomatic of the way people have always responded to *Waiting for Godot*. From the time Beckett's play thrilled and confounded its first audiences, it has invariably provoked passionate responses inside and out of the theatre, both from those who admired it and those who found it tedious or objectionable. When Bertolt Brecht came across a copy of *Warten auf Godot* in 1953, he was so challenged by Beckett's enigmatic stance that he began to sketch what he called a *Gegenentwurf*, a counterdraft or adversarial design, which he hoped would result in a new version of the play. In his notes for a Marxist answer to Beckett, Brecht conceives of Estragon as the proletarian, Vladimir the intellectual, Von Pozzo a landed aristocrat, and poor Lucky a policeman or a fool. The metaphysical overtones are diminished and lines are transferred from one character to another in order to fill in the obligatory social outlines. Vladimir (the poet in Brecht's recasting) falls asleep and the more kindly Estragon refrains from waking him, while he, instead of his friend, confronts Pozzo. To counter Beckett's stark determinism, Brecht alters Estragon's question 'Wir sind doch nicht gebunden?' [We're not tied?] to 'Wir sind natürlich auch an nichts gebunden! [Of course, we're not tied to anything!] And several other changes in these polemical directions followed.

Unfortunately, Brecht abandoned his *Gegenentwurf* at an early stage. Some time later, just before his death in 1956, he considered a production in which films of revolutionary action in Russia, China, Asia, and Africa were to be juxtaposed with the static behaviour of Beckett's two tramps, but this plan also remained abortive. Thus what might have been a memorable 'encounter' between the imaginations of two of the dominant theatrical innovators of the century regrettably never took place.

Not long after Brecht toyed with the idea of having his Berliner Ensemble confront a play he concluded to be reactionary, another troupe performed *Godot* under conditions that revealed its radical nature, and the event has since become one of the great legends of modern theatre history. Although the story of the San Francisco Actors Workshop production at San Quentin penitentiary in 1957 has been told many times (most notably by Martin Esslin to begin his famous *Theatre of the Absurd*), it must always be featured in any account of what is now known as 'the myth of *Godot*'. As Esslin tells it, the company was understandably apprehensive about importing such an obscure and controversial work into so novel an environment; the last live production to appear in the prison had featured Sarah Bernhardt in 1913, and *Godot* was chosen in part because it had no women in the cast. Before the show started, Herbert Blau, the director, suggested to the fourteen-hundred inmates that they respond to *Godot* the way they might to a piece of jazz, listening for whatever might have personal meaning.

The convicts were rapt and warmly received Beckett's imprisoned characters whose plight they could acknowledge as their own. Afterwards their responses were tellingly precise. Godot, one told a reporter afterwards, is society. 'He's the outside' another added. The writer of a review in the prison newspaper put it this way:

It was an expression, symbolic in order to avoid all personal error, by an author who expected each member of the audience to draw his own conclusions, make his own errors. It asked nothing in point, it forced no dramatized moral on the viewer, it held out no specific hope. . . . We're still waiting for Godot, and shall continue to wait. When the scenery gets too drab and the action too slow, we'll call each other names and swear to part forever − but then, there's no place to go!　　　　　(Graver and Federman, pp. 111, 113)

One of the members of that original audience was a twenty-four-year-old Chicago-born prisoner named Rick Cluchy, who was serving a life sentence for (in Ruby Cohn's summary) having kidnapped, shot at, and robbed a hotel executive while under the effect of drugs, although the unharmed victim had pleaded on his behalf. *Waiting for Godot* was the first play Cluchy had ever seen, and it was to change his life. He and several other inmates asked the authorities for permission to set up a theatre workshop and to put on plays for the other convicts. Permission was granted and over the next decade the troupe mounted nearly two dozen shows, including Beckett's *Endgame, Krapp's Last Tape*, and *Act Without Words II*. In 1961, they invited the San Francisco Actor's Workshop back to see the local version of *Godot*, with Cluchy as Vladimir.

From then on, theatre was to be Cluchy's life in prison and out. When he was unexpectedly released on parole in 1966, he returned to Chicago and soon formed the San Quentin Drama Workshop, again concentrating on plays by Beckett. Word of his work reached Europe and the troupe was invited to perform at the Edinburgh Festival and on the Continent. Seeing Beckett on a Paris street, Cluchy introduced himself and the two men became friends and over the next decade occasional collaborators. Under Beckett's direction and on his own, Cluchy acted in *Godot, Endgame*, and *Krapp's Last Tape* in

Europe and America. In 1988, with John Fuegi and Mitchell Lifton of the University of Maryland, he embarked on a substantial project to film the San Quentin group in the three major plays as originally directed by Beckett. When completed, these are likely to be the most widely seen versions of Beckett's work ever produced. For thirty-five years, Beckett had refused permission to adapt *Godot* for the cinema, although he had been approached for permission many times. Once, in 1967, when he received a proposal from Roman Polanski for a version that would feature his friend Jack MacGowran, he wrote to the actor: 'I'm terribly sorry to disappoint you and Polanski but I don't want any film of *Godot*. As it stands it is simply not cinema material. And adaptation would destroy it. Please forgive me . . . and don't think of me as a purist bastard' (Young, p. 120). But since the San Quentin project will be a record of a performance not an adaptation, it does not violate the playwright's principle.

The legendary performances for convicts and by convicts have their analogues in other notable productions of *Godot* for audiences that have known something about the oppressiveness of waiting and of being without power. *Godot* was done with all black casts in New York in 1957 and in Johannesburg in 1962 (Athol Fugard directing) and 1981 (by the Baxter Theatre Company of Cape Town). In Warsaw in 1956, the play was interpreted as a parable of the future emancipation of Poland from the domination of Russia; in Algeria, when that country was still a possession of France, it was understood to be about the much-desired distribution of land to the peasants. In Melbourne in 1976, Vladimir and Estragon appeared as 'no-hopers' wandering the Australian outback where Pozzo was the colonial oppressor and Lucky his enslaved aboriginal. In the late 1970s, Sidney Homan took his Bacchus production to ten prisons across the state of Florida. And in 1986, a cast of prisoners caused a stir by escaping while performing the play in Sweden. That *Godot* should be performed again and again in prisons quite nicely fits Beckett's own sentiments about the work. He once told the journalist Alden Whitman that 'the true *Godot* was the one produced in a

German prison, with the convicts as actors. They [and the audience] understood that 'Godot' is hope, 'Godot' is life — aimless, but always with an element of hope' (*New York Times*, 24 October 1969, p. 32).

But if *Waiting for Godot* has captivated spectators off the main theatrical line, it has been performed, too, in celebrated productions at many of the major theatres of the world: at the Odéon in Paris in 1961; at London's Royal Court in 1964, in Beckett's own production at the Schiller Theater in Berlin in 1975, versions of which later toured in England, America, and Australia; at the National Theatre in London in 1987, and at Lincoln Center in New York in 1988 (to note only a handful). Two graphic comments on Royal Court productions a dozen years apart catch something of the excitement the play was generating. Reviewing Anthony Page's widely praised production (with Nicol Williamson, Jack MacGowran, Paul Curren, and Alfred Lynch), the *Times* critic concluded:

When we first saw *Godot* in London, the play was obviously recognizable as a work of the highest originality and talent; nine years later, it stands revealed as the work that gave the theatre a new language and created a world of its own which has passed into folklore: these are the highest achievements within the range of literary composition, and they establish its greatness as a matter of more than personal opinion.   (*The Times*, 31 December 1964)

Twelve years later, Peter Hall, the director and theatre manager, made this note in his diary:

To the Royal Court to see Sam Beckett's Schiller Theater production in German of *Waiting for Godot*. This is a masterpiece. Absolute precision, clarity, hardness. No sentimentality, no indulgence, no pretension. The ghost of Buster Keaton hovers over Estragon and Vladimir. Vladimir very tall. Estragon small, comic, and heartbreaking: a very great performance this. The production is also quite, quite beautiful. It revived my shaken faith in the theatre.

(J. Goodwin, ed., p. 230)

Because of the playwright's association with the production, the Berlin *Godot* has itself become something of a legend in the contemporary theatre. Beckett had previously directed *Endgame*, *Happy Days*, and *Krapp's Last Tape* at the Schiller, and he came again in late December 1974 to spend ten weeks rehearsing the cast before the première on 7 March. Although he had advised others on earlier productions, he had never directed *Godot* himself, and he shared with friends his feeling that the play (written more than twenty-five years ago) was 'a mess'. As he was accustomed to do when he directed in Berlin, Beckett had already committed the German text to memory and prepared an elaborate set of jottings and sketches in his *Production Notebook* (to be published in 1989 by Faber & Faber). Here he described his goal: 'Der Konfusion Gestalt geben' [To give form to the confusion]. He had also made some revisions and cuts in Elmar Tophoven's German translation, bringing it closer to his own, trimmed English version, which he preferred as the performance text of the play (Tophoven's German text is based on the original French).

Most striking in the *Production Notebook* are hundreds of descriptions and diagrams about gesture, movement, position, and balance reflecting Beckett's desire to create a strong visual and spatial effect for this production of a play he once complained had not been sufficiently visualized. Some of the notable choices and changes that the playwright made for this production have already been described in chapter two (resisting a discussion of the play's general themes, articulating the concept of the caged dynamic in physical terms, adding 'red' to Vladimir's question about the colour of Godot's beard, and beginning the rehearsals with Lucky's tirade). The great majority of other choices had to do with matters of symmetry and repetition designed to highlight the way people use their bodies to help pass the time and to relate to one another. In the hands of the author turned director, the play became more rhythmical and formal than it had ever been before. In his notebook, Beckett broke down the action into 109 units of waiting; and in day-to-day rehearsals with the actors, he continually emphasized the importance of the way characters came together and separated, and how they were joined and isolated. Particular attention was given to forming cruciform patterns and images of semi-circles, arcs, chords, and triangles to reinforce the sense of the various temporary and incomplete orders people can create within the fixed figure of the circle in which they are encaged. James Knowlson has noted that in the San Quentin production supervised by Beckett in 1984, the same cruciform images prevail, and they are clearly set in the context of 'a long drawn-out martyrdom where the painful waiting is relieved by fewer and less animated "little canters" than in the Berlin production of nine years earlier. Balletic vaudeville numbers have become a few tired "wriggles" as the nails go in' ('Beckett as Director', p. 460).

The emphasis on linking and symbiosis was also evident in the costuming. As was mentioned earlier, not only did Vladimir wear striped trousers, which fit him, with Estragon's black jacket, which didn't, but Estragon wore black trousers with his friend's striped jacket which was too big for him. Lucky's shoes were the same colour as Pozzo's hat, and his checked waistcoat and grey trousers complemented those of his master. With his customary meticulousness, Beckett also emphasized the musical and ritual elements in his conception of the play (analogy, repetition, leitmotifs), even going so far as to add tunes from Chopin's 'Funeral March' and Franz Lehár's 'Merry Widow Waltz' to Vladimir's dog song. Directing the falling sequence in Act II, he instructed the actor playing Lucky not to fall realistically but in a stylized way. When asked if there was to be no naturalism whatever, he replied: 'It is a game, everything is a game. When all four of them are lying on the ground, that cannot be handled naturalistically. That has got to be done artificially, with beauty, like ballet. Otherwise, everything becomes only an imitation of reality.' And to the question 'Should it take on a dryness?' he answered: 'It should become clear and transparent, not dry. It is a game in order to survive' (Walter Asmus, quoted on p. 140 of Martha Fehsenfeld's and Dougald McMillan's *Beckett in the Theatre*, which has a valuable detailed account of the 1975 Schiller Theater production).

Godot and the popular imagination

The survival game that began in the 1950s as a *succès de scandale* had become not long after one of the most celebrated and influential dramatic works in the history of the theatre. Now performed regularly in dozens of languages around the world, it has been hailed not only by playwrights as an artistic liberation, but by millions of spectators and readers as a work of extraordinary force and beauty that expresses the most vital of contemporary and universal concerns.

In addition to the iconoclastic *Godot* quickly becoming a theatre classic, it also (as the *Times* reviewer pointed out) entered with equal swiftness into the language of common speech. In October 1955, long before the play appeared in Ireland, an *Irish Times* cartoon showed a Dublin policeman about to arrest a tramp lying under a tree, and remarking: 'I'm afraid this is going to be no run-of-the-mill vagrancy case – he claims he's the Reclining Figure waiting for Godot . . .' Not long after, during a crisis in the government of Harold Macmillan, the cartoonist Vicky depicted the prime minister as Vladimir and one of his cabinet colleagues as Estragon, mournfully contemplating a newspaper headline about 'Budget Hopes' and declaring 'We'll hang ourselves tomorrow . . . Unless Godot comes.' Someone named Vladimir Estragon now writes the culinary column, 'Waiting for Dessert', for the *Village Voice* newspaper in New York (reasonable enough, since 'estragon' is French for 'tarragon'). In 1987, after the American congressional hearings about the so-called Iran-Contra scandal, the *New York Times* columnist, Tom Wicker, wrote a piece titled 'Godot Isn't Coming' to warn the field of Democratic presidential hopefuls that the ideal candidate was unlikely to appear at the last moment. And the popular American cartoonist, Gary Trudeau, in his strip 'Doonesbury', satirized Mario Cuomo's reluctance to announce his decision about running for the highest office by drawing two men near a tree on a country road. They are told by a boy that the awaited Mr Cuomo (both of whose names are teasingly close to Godot) is 'in Moscow again,' a message that provokes the speculation that 'perhaps he could be defecting'.

Other important evidence of the widespread familiarity of *Godot* comes from the world of spoof and parody. The Yugoslavian writer, Miodrag Bulatović, achieved some notoriety in 1966 with *Godo je dosao*, (*Godot Has Arrived*), a play written in Serbo-Croatian, translated into German and French, and performed in cities around Germany and in Sweden. Bulotović's Godot materializes as a baker who brings bread to a starving populace. After various misadventures, Beckett's characters condemn him to death, but he is declared non-existent by Lucky and departs, leaving sacks of flour for posterity. Bulatović calls his work a play of ideas (like Brecht's sketch, in opposition to *Godot*), but it is more interesting as tendency than theatre. More successful by common report is Roland Dubillard's cabaret sketch, 'Waiting for Grouchy', which fools with borrowings from Beckett that he was depending on his audience to recognize.

In cartoons, newspapers, magazines, night clubs, and television shows, the words and images of *Godot* are now as common and recognizable as images from Picasso, Kafka, T. S. Eliot, Giacometti, or Joyce.

Godot and the contemporary theatre

If *Waiting for Godot* has become a familiar presence in daily life, in the contemporary theatre it is something more akin to a presiding spirit. In her book on the French texts of Beckett's two best-known works, J.P. Little provides a compact description of just how thoroughly *Godot* has been absorbed into the theatre of our time.

Almost everything recognisably 'modern' owes a debt to *Godot*: Arrabal, Stoppard, Albee, Pinter, to mention only some of the best-known, are, in Martin Esslin's words, all 'children of Godot.' The sense of the play being a landmark, conveyed by William Saroyan when he said that Godot would 'make it easier for me and everyone else to write freely in the theatre' is precisely what makes us accept it now as the norm.

(*En attendant Godot and Fin de Partie*, pp. 11–12)

The paradox is fascinating. The great playwright of not-knowing and not-being-able has been the most fertile, liberating influence in the contemporary theatre, indeed, less an influence than an inspiration. That influence is now, of course, based not only on one play but on thirty-two, on half a dozen major works of fiction, and on his reputation as a writer of exemplary dedication and imaginative resourcefulness. But since it was with *Godot* that Beckett made his first and most powerful impact, and since that play is our subject, we will continue in this brief survey to focus primarily on *its* afterlife.

The best of his successors do not borrow from Beckett, nor do they write works that are derivative. They perceive in his radical reductions a surprisingly rich set of invitations to explore further their own emotional and intellectual concerns and to expand their technical means for dramatizing them. Not only playwrights, but directors, actors, and designers often talk of 'absorbing Beckett', of 'going through Beckett', of translating him into their own idiom. It is the playwrights, though, who have registered Beckett's influence most memorably. Chief among them is Harold Pinter, who has always been forthright and generous about his esteem for the man he called, as early as 1954, 'far and away the finest writer writing'. 'There is no question', Pinter once told a television interviewer, 'that Beckett is a writer whom I admire very much and have admired for a number of years. If Beckett's influence shows in my work that's all right with me. You don't write in a vacuum; you're bound to absorb and digest other writing and I admire Beckett's work so much that something of its texture might appear in my own' ('Harold Pinter Replies', BBC Third Programme, (1963).

Not only the textures but the structural configurations of Pinter's early plays are reminiscent of Beckett (and not only of *Godot* but of the novels, *Endgame*, *Krapp's Last Tape*, and the radio plays). Many of Pinter's plays have actions built around a pregnant absence: the motive behind the torture of Stanley by Goldberg and McCann in *The Birthday Party* (1958) or behind the manipulation of Davies by Mick and Aston in *The Caretaker* (1960); or the effect of the dead

Jessie on the house she haunts in *The Homecoming* (1965). In *The Dumb Waiter* (1960), the hired assassins, Ben and Gus, wait alone in a room for the arrival of a victim who never appears; they receive enigmatic messages they cannot decipher; they talk mysteriously about their boss who never shows up; and they are unable to determine who operates the clattering dumb waiter that so surprisingly descends with requests for fancy food. While waiting for the murder that doesn't occur, Gus and Ben pass the time asking rapid-fire questions, telling stories, and performing ritual gestures that in their humour and suggestiveness seem like homage to Beckett. Pinter begins *The Dumb Waiter* with a delicate mime that slyly combines the best gestures of Gogo *and* Didi. First seen straining to tie the laces of one shoe, Gus then takes off the other shoe, peers into it, recovers a flattened matchbox, puts the shoe back on, ties it, takes off the other one, peers into it, and comes up with a cigarette packet. The comic mix of assiduity and seriousness tells the audience something important about his personality and prepares us for the disquieting role of questioner that he will later play.

Many of the rituals and routines in Pinter's plays could with few alterations fit handsomely in Beckett's: Stanley and McCann whistling 'The Mountains of Morne', Mick tantalizing Davies with the handbag, Gus and Ben quarrelling about whether one should say 'light the kettle' or 'light the gas', or Ben grilling Gus in the killer's catechism. And the closing lines of the sadistic interrogation of Stanley is a patterned variation on the first of Vladimir's and Estragon's exchanges about Godot:

GOLDBERG: You'll be integrated
McCANN: You'll give orders.
GOLDBERG: You'll make decisions.
McCANN: You'll be a magnate.
GOLDBERG: A statesman.
McCANN: You'll own yachts.
GOLDBERG: Animals.
McCANN: Animals.   (Act III)

Pinter's most inspired monologues often work like Lucky's

tirade. Goldberg running on about his uncle Barney, Davies recalling an abusive encounter with a monk near Luton, Mick on the bloke he once knew in Shoreditch, Aston on getting shock treatment, Lenny on beating a prostitute down by the docks – underneath what is said in all these startling set-pieces something else is being said, and it always has to do with the major themes of the play. Some of Pinter's characters seem like figures from *Godot* living in another place. Goldberg, for instance, could well be Pozzo transplanted from the manor to a boarding house in an English seaside town. His set-pieces on his old mum and on getting up in the morning have the sinister provocation of Pozzo's description of what our local twilights can do. And Goldberg's vaunting speech about his own fitness that so shockingly ends with his collapse into the void mirrors Pozzo's dissolution in the second act of *Godot* ('Because I believe that the world . . . (*Vacant*.) . . . Because I believe that the world . . . (*Desperate*.) . . . BECAUSE I BELIEVE THAT THE WORLD . . . (*Lost*.)').

Pinter's theatre language also has qualities in common with Beckett's. His linguistic aim, he once said, 'is stringency, shading, accuracy', and in *The Caretaker* and *The Homecoming* the brutal, distressing subject-matter is expressed in an elegant, often richly cadenced prose. Similarly, the two playwrights are masters of the disturbing *non sequitur*. Here, for instance, is a double-take that has the Beckett self-cancelling stamp on it:

GOLDBERG: McCann, what are you so nervous about? Pull yourself together. Everywhere you go these days it's like a funeral.
McCANN: That's true.
GOLDBERG: True? Of course it's true. It's more than true. It's a fact.
McCANN: You may be right.   (Act I)

Pinter's plays, like Beckett's, also invite and resist allegory simultaneously. *The Dumb Waiter* can be read as a fable about two functionaries employed to commit murder in a highly-organized technological society. *The Birthday Party* has the shape of a ritual interrogation and torture of a non-conformist; and in *The Caretaker* seedy characters appear to be enacting some myth about power, territory, exclusion and expulsion. Yet in each case these readings turn out to be in important ways reductive; the plays, again like *Godot*, elude such singular definition. We may be drawn in by the seductiveness of many possible allegories, but no single one will satisfactorily encompass the play's richness of implication.

Yet for all these echoes and similarities, the essential fact about Pinter's work is how fundamentally different it is from Beckett's. All of his early plays are located in a gritty, realistic English setting: 'The Dumb Waiter' in Birmingham, *The Birthday Party* in a seaside resort town, *The Caretaker* in the west of London and *The Homecoming* in the city's north; and his characters are usually 'located' as well, either by details about their activities or by their vernacular speech. Although Pinter's plays use ritual and myth to enact fundamental dramas of existence, they are more social and circumstantial, less metaphysical than Beckett's, and the striking speech patterns of his people are shaped more by the pressure of individual psychology and class. In Pinter, games do not exist to pass the time, but rather to reveal the erotic and often intimidating nature of power in contemporary society, the way personal alliances form, break down and take surprising new shapes. The atmosphere of menace so palpable in his plays is less the threat of non-being (as it is in Beckett's) than of being expelled from a communal context the characters would like to believe is secure. Our bafflement in watching a Pinter play is not primarily a matter of the universe being mysterious or of God being absent, but rather of our not being able to establish plausible reasons why the people speak and behave as cryptically as they do. Beckett's Krapp says 'Never knew such silence. The earth might be uninhabited'; Pinter's Max remarks 'You never heard such silence' – the cosmic chilliness of the first and the discomforting tautological humour of the second are differentiating marks of the two playwrights. Overall, Beckett and Pinter write very different kinds of comedy. In *Godot*, the humour comes primarily from the cabaret and music hall, and when it is used to express ironic perceptions of being and non-being the result is Beckett's unique kind of elegantly austere tragi-comedy. Pinter in contrast writes an updated version of seventeenth-century comedy of manners: plays in which a stylized mix of the ferocious and the debonair exposes the brutal realities beneath the familiar surface of modern social life.

Like Pinter, Tom Stoppard has also been frequently direct and characteristically witty in his admiration for Beckett's plays and novels. 'There are certain things written in English', he once said, 'which make me feel as a diabetic must when the insulin goes in. Prufrock and Beckett are the twin syringes of my diet, my arterial system' (Hayman, p. 8). Stoppard's very first attempt at writing for the theatre was a one-act play called *The Gamblers* (1960), which he later described in a letter to Kenneth Tynan as '*Waiting for Godot* in the death cell – prisoner and jailer – I'm sure you can imagine the rest' (*The New Yorker*, 19 December 1977, p. 51). *Rosencrantz and Guildenstern Are Dead* (1967), the comedy that made Stoppard famous, is a perfect illustration of how he has successfully used Beckett for his own creative purposes.

When the action starts, Hamlet's school friends (classic emblems of insignificance) are alone 'in a place without any visible character', routinely tossing coins and chatting about memory, habit, happiness, the law of probability, and how to pass the time. In his pragmatic, intuitive nature, Rosencrantz is the Estragon figure (Ros/Gogo), while Guildenstern, the more inquiring and speculative of the pair resembles Vladimir (Guil/Didi); and together they are the halves of a couple, two sides of the coins they so obsessively toss. While the solitary courtiers try to figure out what is happening to them, they engage in conversational volleys the source of which is often unmistakable:

GUIL: Then what are we doing here, I ask myself.
ROS: You might well ask.
GUIL: We better get on.
ROS: You might well think.
GUIL: We better get on.
ROS: (*actively*): Right! (*Pause.*) On where?

'Beckett gives me more pleasure than I can express', Stoppard once said, 'because he always ends up with a man surrounded by the wreckage of a proposition he had made in confidence only two minutes before' (*Sunday Times*, 25 February 1968, p. 47).

Stoppard's veneration of Beckett is obvious in many other verbal and visual echoes throughout the play. The leader of the travelling troupe has Pozzo's flamboyant ability to take centre stage and to command his company with the charge 'On-ward!'; and when Ros and Guil try to slow Hamlet's movements by hooking their belts together, Ros's pants predictably drop to his ankles. In the tradition of Vladimir reflecting on the two thieves, Rosencrantz tells how 'two early Christians chanced to meet in Heaven. "Saul of Tarsus yet!" cried one. "What are *you* doing here?" . . . 'Tarsus-Schmarsus", replied the other, "I'm Paul already" ' – a joke that serves Stoppard's own deflationary purposes very well, but does not move into a more serious area of discourse, the way Beckett's image does. Bishop Berkeley twice makes his obligatory appearance: first, when the Player laments the humiliation of the actor tricked out of the 'single assumption which makes our existence viable – that somebody is *watching*'; and then later when Rosencrantz yells 'fire' in order to demonstrate the misuse of free speech, a nice spoof of *esse est percipi*. And Guildenstern pays tribute to Vladimir paying tribute to Hamlet when he says 'Words, words. They're all we have to go on.' Perhaps the most memorable of Stoppard's appropriations of Beckett – the breath-taking barrel routine at the end of Act III – comes of course not from *Godot*, but out of the ash cans of *Endgame* and the urns of *Play*.

But what frees Stoppard from the charge of being merely derivative is his ability to turn one of Beckett's central subjects to his own unique advantage. Rosencrantz and Guildenstern are Estragon and Vladimir at a later state of their epistemological dilemma. Although they, too, are baffled innocents who have little understanding of their roles in a world that is of someone else's making, they are more cosmopolitan than their counterparts, more aware of their own belatedness, though not of its source. Caught not only in someone else's world but also in someone else's play, they are hostages to *Hamlet* just as Didi and Gogo are hostages to Godot.

What it means to be hostages to *Hamlet* is Stoppard's own subject and he explores it with an originality that makes his play as distinctive as Beckett's (if obviously, as he himself would be the first to say, of smaller dimensions). Vladimir and Estragon are faced with a mysterious obligation: they must wait for Godot, and there is no suggestion of any coherent explanation of why they do what they do. Their inability to understand what is happening to them (except in terms of a mysterious obligation) is shared by the audience, and the mutual incomprehension and persistence of the characters *and* the audience is at the heart of the bleak beauty of Beckett's play. Stoppard's play works very differently, for there is a fundamental split between what the protagonists and the audience know. Rosencrantz and Guildenstern never understand that the context in which their fates are being decided is the intrigue of the Danish court and the moral and psychological predicament of the Prince – perhaps the best-known theatrical plot ever contrived. All the ironies of *Rosencrantz and Guildenstern are Dead* – trivial and substantial – rest on this fundamental disjunction. But if the protagonists do not know they are doomed functionaries in a play called *Hamlet*, they are aware of the general implications of their plight: the uncertainty of identity, existence in a universe of unanswerable questions, the mysteries of birth and death. This second split – of not knowing the specific facts but being only too well aware of the abstract ones – is the source of the comedy and the compassion with which Stoppard treats the two courtiers.

There is at first something consoling as well as entertaining for the audience in the ignorance of Ros and Guil, for we are comfortably in on the joke from which they are fatally excluded. There *is* a providence in the fall of a sparrow, and the providential agent is Shakespeare, who wrote the play that gave mayhem, murder, and anguish its immortal and meaningful shape. The secret that Stoppard shares with us is that only art creates order, and there is no match for the force and beauty of its process. But there is a surprising, disquieting turn to this. By getting us to look at this most familiar of plays from a fresh standpoint, Stoppard makes us ask questions about our previous understanding: not only about how we are to take the celebrated nonentities, but also the most eminent of tragic heroes. How well, for instance, did Hamlet understand his two school friends and was he unnecessarily vicious in dispatching them? Once we ask this we have to wonder if we have correctly understood the plot of *Hamlet* in the first place; and then go one step further: to conceive of the possibility that we, too, may be uncomprehending actors in the prefigured events of our own lives.

Stoppard's design rests on Beckett's achievement, but it has its own impressive originality. The play operates brilliantly on at least two levels: as a theatrical comedy that turns the most famous English tragedy inside out and as a universal drama about the inability of human beings to understand the forces directing their own lives. Stoppard views his two victims with ironic humour and compassion (just as Beckett views Didi and Gogo); and he gets a late twentieth-century audience to perceive these Renaissance flounderers as men imprisoned in an incomprehensible universe that unexpectedly reflects our own.

In Stoppard's other early major play, *Jumpers* (1972), there are also debts to Beckett, one very general, the other entirely specific. In this sparkling ideological farce, Stoppard pits his hero, George Moore, a befuddled but sympathetic humanist professor of moral philosophy, against the formidably adroit proponents of logical positivism. The central debate is woven through a whodunit plot (replete with a strip-tease and acrobats) that turns on the murder of a gymnast, the hijinks of Moore's neurasthenic wife (a retired music-hall singer), the election of the ultra-rational Red-Lib party, the appointment of an atheist cabinet minister as Archbishop of Canterbury, and more madcap goings-on than are likely to have been dreamt of in anyone's philosophy before. The endearingly zany Moore moves through the craziness trying to prove the existence of ethical absolutes, while his adversary, the suave vice-chancellor of the university, Sir Archibald Jumper, puts forth a pragmatic materialist point of view.

The play ends with a dream sequence in which Moore addresses a university symposium on the subject 'Man – good, bad, or indifferent?' and Jumper, who throughout has been a devilishly elusive figure, closes the debate and the play itself with a parody of two of the most famous speeches from *Waiting for Godot*.

Do not despair – many are happy much of the time; more eat than starve, more are healthy than sick, more curable than dying; not so many dying as dead; and one of the thieves was saved. Hell's bells and all's well – half the world is at peace with itself, and so is the other half; vast areas are unpolluted; millions of children grow up without suffering deprivation, and millions, while deprived, grow up without suffering cruelties, and millions, while deprived and cruelly treated, none the less grow up. No laughter is sad and many tears are joyful. At the graveside the undertaker doffs his top hat and impregnates the prettiest mourner. Wham, bam, thank you Sam.

(*Jumpers*, Coda)

Hilarious on its face, Stoppard's parody works splendidly for him in several ways. No theatre audience could fail to respond with delight at a playwright's closing a philosophical farce with so amusing a send-up of the most famous thematic lines in modern drama. But the parody is an incisive piece of characterization as well. Throughout the play, Sir Archie has been offering cunningly cultivated defences of amoral positions. Here, he uses language originally meant to express uncertainty and despair to embody a cynical defence of rational accommodation. But given the events of the last part of the play and the appealing, if clownish, sincerity of Moore, Sir Archie sounds like a trendy version of Voltaire's Dr Pangloss, using a refined wit to claim that all is for the best in a world that *Jumpers* portrays as a riotous version of *Endgame*. His expert parody of Beckett doubly reveals his insensitivity to deprivation and suffering, and gives the audience's final verdict to Moore. In this context, Sir Archie's clever 'wham, bam, thank you Sam' is counterfeit, but Stoppard's parodic tribute turns out to be genuine and heartfelt.

If Beckett has served as a progenitor for Pinter and Stoppard, he has also opened up new theatrical possibilities for many other contemporary writers and directors. For the South African Athol Fugard, for instance, Beckett has been both an inspiration and a goad. In the late 1950s and early 1960s, when he was writing *The Blood Knot* and the other plays that were to establish his reputation, Fugard often read and performed Beckett as a stimulus to his own creative activity. In late December of 1962, after finishing *Malone Dies*, he confided to his notebook:

Hard to describe what this book, like his *Godot*, *Krapp*, and *Endgame*, did to me. Moved? Horrified? Depressed? Elated? Yes, and excited. I wanted to start writing again the moment I put it down. Beckett's greatness doesn't intimidate me. I don't know how it works − but he makes me want to work. Everything of his I have read has done this − I suppose it's because I really understand, emotionally, and this cannot but give me power and energy and faith.
(*Notebooks*, p. 67)

Earlier that same year, Fugard had directed a production of *Godot* with a black cast in Johannesburg, and he came away feeling that he 'had made contact with the rare moment of truth in theatre . . . truth at the level where it is Beauty'. What he had found in Beckett was above all a writer who had made noble, stirring art from the dismal facts of contemporary history. Vladimir and Estragon, Fugard told his actors, 'must have read the accounts of the Nuremberg trials − or else they were at Sharpeville, or were the first in at Auschwitz. Choose your horror − they know all about it' (*Notebooks*, p. 62).

Echoes of Beckett are easy to locate in Fugard's early plays. The two brothers in *The Blood Knot* (1961) − one light-skinned the other dark − are complementary halves of a whole, and they spend the entire play in routines of dominance and submission, wishing for different versions of a future they will never have. Here, as elsewhere in Fugard, there is moving talk about the nature and limits of human endurance. Pozzo's 'Isn't that enough for you?' is an echoing refrain. In addition to the thematic parallels, there is a shared interest in contrapuntal structure. Fugard, like Beckett, often speaks of the great composers when he describes his aims as a playwright. 'I have learnt more about writing plays from Bach', he once said, 'than from anything I've read by a writer outside of Samuel Beckett' (*Plays and Players*, November 1973, p. 37). But more important than these obvious parallels is the way that confronting Beckett turned out to be a creative stimulus for Fugard. The most telling illustration is the gripping *Boesman and Lena*, first produced at the Rhodes University Little Theatre, Grahamstown, in July 1969.

On the surface, *Boesman and Lena* could hardly be more Beckettian. The action begins with a middle-aged coloured man staggering on to an empty stage burdened with all his material possessions: an old mattress and blanket, a few tins and utensils, and a piece of corrugated iron. Moments later, a coloured woman enters carrying her load on her head. As they talk, we learn that this destitute couple had been driven earlier that day from their shack at Korsten when the whites demolished the shantytown there, and they plan to build a shelter for the night here in the mudflats of the Swartkops river estuary, a few miles from Port Elizabeth. When the exhausted Lena says 'I want my life. Where's it?' Boesman replies, 'In the mud, where you are, *Now*. Tomorrow it will be there too, and the next day.' The rest of the play consists of their good and bad-humoured talk about past and present calamities and their enigmatic encounter with an old black man who appears from nowhere to share their fire. After Boesman's vicious beating of Lena and his kicking the corpse of the old man (whose death passed unobserved), they again take up their burdens and at the play's end trudge into the darkness. Like Vladimir and Estragon, Boesman and Lena are – in antagonism, need, affection, and loyalty – permanently tied together, 'victims of a common predicament – and of each other'.

Yet despite the many similarities to *Godot* and *Endgame*, *Boesman and Lena* is a work of considerable freshness and power, and it is possible now (thanks to the publication of

Fugard's *Notebooks 1960–1977*) to get an unusual glimpse into the process by which he worked with and against Beckett to create a play very much his own. The impulse to follow Beckett is obvious in Fugard's observation that the predicament of Boesman and Lena interests him not on a social or political level, but metaphysically, as a metaphor of the human condition 'which revolution or legislation cannot substantially change'. In other notes, he echoes Beckett on the importance of dramatizing tension through stark visual and aural imagery, and of the need to create a strong sense throughout of 'ontological insecurity'. Without referring to Berkeley or to Beckett, he even speaks of Lena's 'demand that her life be witnessed', a major theme of the play, and an echo not only of Vladimir but of Winnie in *Happy Days*. In one extended notebook entry summarizing his aims as a writer, Fugard proposes an existential theatre in which we confront 'the Nothingness of space and silence with our Being', and try 'to take the desperation out of Silence' by learning to live with it, and to 'think of it as something real and positive – not "nothing" or negative'.

But along with the evidence suggesting Fugard's commitment to a Beckettian theatre, there are a dozen entries in which he can be seen working to heighten the circumstantial realism of his play. He sketches half a dozen men and women around Port Elizabeth who provided images of courage amidst destitution that helped him make his characters more life-like and vivid. He remarks on the need to give Boesman and Lena greater psychological depth and sociological validity by being concrete about self-loathing, shame, disgust, dominance and submission, and the desire for independence. In one entry, Fugard even provides a detailed list of the real places where his fictional characters walked and worked and lived, admitting that (as Lena puts it) this explains nothing, but that he himself had reached a point 'where I needed to know'. And there are several striking comments that reveal Fugard in the act of asserting the primacy of his own affirmative naturalism. He observes that the unrelieved physical and spiritual squalor of the situation 'demands that I write this one more "beautifully" than ever before. "Flowers on the rubbish heap." ' Boesman's predicament is described in terms of the emasculation of manhood by the South African way of life, 'guilt, prejudice and fear, all conspiring together finally to undermine the ability to love directly and forth-rightly'. Then, in an eloquent statement of intention, he first wonders about how he might align himself with forces of social change even though he has no clear image of what the future might look like, and he concludes with a definition of the social content of the play: 'Nagging doubts that I am opting out on this score, that I am not saying enough. At one level their predicament is an indictment of this society which makes people "rubbish". Is this explicit enough?' Finally, two years after writing the play, Fugard provides a summary that can be read as a declaration of independence: 'This experience still so vivid in my writing of *Boesman and Lena* where the Truth becomes bigger than self — where I moved from "artifice" to "witnessing" — with all the compulsion, urgency, moral imperative of that role.'

Although perhaps not so deliberately, many other writers can be said to have translated *Godot* into their own idioms. Sam Shepard's first play, *Cowboys #2* (1967), reflects a fascination with Beckett's situation and techniques. As Shepard once explained, a friend in California tossed a copy of a book on his lap, and 'I started reading this play he gave me, and it was like nothing I'd ever read before — it was *Waiting for Godot*. And I thought, what's this guy talking about, what is this? And I read it with a very keen interest, but I didn't know anything about what it *was*' (Brienza, p. 180).

Shephard obviously knew enough of what *Godot* was to use it effectively for his own purposes. *Cowboys #2* opens with two men in black pants, shirts, vests, and hats sitting on a sawhorse, the only prop on a dimly-lit, bare stage, and an inanimate descendant of Beckett's emblematic tree. They pass the time in talk about the weather, imitate old cowboys passing the time talking about the weather, do callisthenics, insult the audience, roll in imaginary mud during a clownish rain dance, engage in skirmishes with non-existent Indians, and deliver manic monologues about the wasteland of American suburbia. At the very close, two anonymous men in business suits (who have been heard off-stage from the start) enter holding scripts and begin to read the text of *Cowboys #2* in dry monotone. Shepard's cowboys are suddenly perceived as distraught figures of uncertain identity, playing roles in a drama of someone else's making, creating routines to cope with a past and a present they cannot otherwise handle. But the routines themselves – full of verbal and physical energy – are very funny (as well as jaggedly disquieting); and as they progress they build to a pointed little parable about American history: the disappearance of the old West, the yearning for pastoral values and heroic possibility, and the blight brought on by technology.

Shepard's contemporary David Mamet has also adapted some of Beckett's most distinctive theatrical techniques to write about a more realistic subject-matter. In such early plays as *Duck Variations* (1971), Mamet imitated Beckett's antiphonal dialogue and musical structure. More recently, he has been adapting Beckett (mediated through Pinter) to write about the chicanery of American business people on the make. Mamet's hustlers, sleazy real-estate agents, and venal Hollywood production people express their desires and grievances by repeating words and phrases, often obscene, in rapid-fire, staccato variations. Beckett's terse lyricism with metaphysical overtones becomes Mamet's gritty, attention-grabbing coarseness. In *Glengarry Glen Ross* (1983) and *Speed-the-Plow* (1987), the mix of vaudeville and Miami Beach night-club banter serves to satirize self-seeking and corruption, but the swift, finely-timed delivery of raucously crude characters has an undeniable force and appeal. Indeed, at times *Speed-the-Plow* even plays as if it might be a sly parody of *Godot*. The two men on stage, Bobby Gould, a new head of production at a Hollywood studio and Charlie Fox, an independent producer, are in hostage to *two* off-stage figures who literally hold their futures in their hands. Gould and Fox engage in long exchanges of crisps, cross-cutting dialogue while they wait to find out if the absent head of the studio will agree to film a sure-fire commercial script with an influential actor or director, whose identity is elusive and who likewise never appears. The discomforting joke at the end is that Godot 'comes': Gould and Fox get their contract. Corruption wins out and male bonding based on venality and aggression is affirmed.

Another telling illustration of just how thoroughly *Godot* has been assimilated into contemporary consciousness is provided by a production in 1979 at the National Theatre of Strasburg. Here, a performance piece called *Ils allaient obscurs sous la nuit solitaire: D'après En attendant Godot de Samuel Beckett*, was staged in an abandoned hangar. On a set consisting of a huge modern urban street scene, ten characters spoke snatches of dialogue from the original French *Godot*. The dominant structures of the fog-gripped, ghostly physical setting were a neon-lit bar, two cars parked at a kerb, three shops (one of which was a dentist's consulting room), and such familiar objects as TV sets, supermarket trolleys and parking meters. The ten characters were named Didi, Gogo, Lucky, Pozzo, the owner of the Citroën, the barman, the bridegroom, the bride, the man with the Ricard (an aperitif), and the man with the club-foot. They spoke the segments of dialogue of *Godot* in discontinuous order and the action was punctuated with acts of brutal violence, most notably a rape and an enormous explosion attributed to terrorists, followed by the cries for help from the second act of the play. The aims of the director, André Engel, and the dramaturg Bernard Pautrat were bold and clear: to offer 'not an original or wiser version of the play, but a faithful, black picture of our time, following the tone set by all of Beckett's works'; and what came across from the production was a striking representation of a technological society in an advanced stage of paralysis and disintegration. (A detailed account of the Strasburg *Godot* is given by Anne C. Murch, pp. 113–29.)

The use here of Beckett's text tells us a good deal about its status as an icon in contemporary culture. First, the director can deploy *Godot* the way Tom Stoppard used *Hamlet* because it is assumed to be so well known as to provide an almost universal frame of reference. Second, Beckett's text is taken as the already classic theatrical formulation of modern anxiety about uncertainty and barrenness in a material world without transcendent purpose. To break *Godot* into pieces and have it spoken by frozen figures who are not waiting *for* anything is to intensify the sense of alienation and fright embodied in the original text. To give characters only Beckett's words in random order is to deny them expression of their own and thus to abandon them to a language that in this context is futureless. So extreme is the sense of atomization in 'Ils allaient obscurs . . .' that Beckett's text functions ironically as a trace, the way the Bible does in *Godot* itself: as the surviving mark of a former civilization that once gave form and coherence to human aspirations. By grafting their work on *Godot*, the Strasburg theatre people seem almost nostalgic for a time when the modern predicament could be formulated as artfully (and as hopefully!) as it was by Beckett.

For one last (if discordant) opinion about the centrality of *Godot*, it is worth mentioning John Peter's polemical book, *Vladimir's Carrot: Modern Drama and the Modern Imagination* (1987). Peter argues that Beckett's work is the epitome of a new kind of modern drama, 'the closed play', in which the audience is deprived of an understanding of the meaning of an action that exists entirely outside a demonstrable historical, social, psychological or moral context. Unlike Clytemnestra's tapestries or Mrs Alving's books (the resonant properties of the *Oresteia* and *Ghosts*), Vladimir's carrot exists in a vacuum, for it tells us virtually nothing about the characters' background or their situation. Starting with this vivid metaphor, Peter goes on to explore the history of modern drama in relation to modern literature and philosophy, using Beckett's play as an example of an immensely influential kind of theatre of which he strongly disapproves. Although he admits that *Waiting for Godot* 'may turn out to be the single most important event in the theatre since Aeschylus', he judges it to be a lamentable and in some ways a potentially dangerous dead end. Although Peter's argument is vigorously pursued, it is founded on a solemn, singular reading of the effects and implications of *Godot*, with which — as this study has argued — nearly all audiences and playwrights are likely to disagree. For if there is now a common consensus about *Godot*, it is that the play is endlessly open and accessible, not only to interpretation but to understanding.

Beckett's play, then, has given much of recent dramatic literature not only its subject-matter — the baffled search for transcendence in a mysterious world that will not yield up its purpose or meaning — but also many of its characteristic modes of presentation: mythical and musical structure, stripped-down iconographic imagery, the blend of humour and metaphysics (the circus and the seminar), and a haunting poetic prose to give desolate aspiration its authentic comic voice. So thoroughly has *Waiting for Godot* been absorbed into the collective imagination of the late twentieth century that its words, images, characters, situations, and themes can now be found just about everywhere. As Alan Schneider aptly put it, *Godot* is in one sense no longer a play but a condition of life.

Guide to further reading

The most accessible editions of Beckett's play are *En attendant Godot*, Editions de Minuit, Paris; and *Waiting for Godot*, Faber & Faber, London and Grove Press, New York. The German edition of *Warten auf Godot*, published by Suhrkamp, Frankfurt, also reprints the French and the English texts.

Waiting for Godot was the first of Beckett's thirty-two plays to be published and performed. *Samuel Beckett: The Complete Dramatic Works*, Faber & Faber, London, 1986, reprints all of his writing for stage, radio, and television in one volume. But the text of *Waiting for Godot* is the expurgated version of 1956 and should not be used.

At present there is no definitive text of the play. For a useful discussion of some of the differences between the English and American editions see Hersh Zeifman, 'The Alterable Whey of Words: The Texts of *Waiting for Godot*', *Educational Theatre Journal*, 29, March 1977, pp. 77–84.

Dougald McMillan has edited *'Waiting for Godot': The Production Notebook*, Faber & Faber, London, 1989.

The citations given below are chosen to provide some sense of the range and diversity of the enormous body of writing about *Waiting for Godot* and Beckett's work in general. Anyone who wishes to read more about the play would profitably begin with the writings of Ruby Cohn, Colin Duckworth, and John Fletcher. All criticism of the play, including this study, is indebted to their pioneering work.

General studies of Beckett

Deirdre Bair, *Samuel Beckett: A Biography*, Cape, London, 1978.
Linda Ben-Zvi, *Samuel Beckett*, Twayne Publishers, Boston, 1986.
Tom Bishop and Raymond Federman, editors, *Cahiers de l'Herne: Samuel Beckett*, L'Herne, Paris, 1976.
Enoch Brater, editor, *Beckett at 80/Beckett in Context*, Oxford University Press, Oxford, 1986.
Why Beckett, Thames & Hudson, London, 1988.
Pierre Chabert, editor, *Samuel Beckett*, special number of *Revue d'Esthétique*, Toulouse, 1986.

Ruby Cohn, *Back to Beckett*, Princeton University Press, Princeton, New Jersey, 1973.

  Just Play: Beckett's Theater, Princeton University Press, Princeton, New Jersey, 1980.

Martin Esslin, editor, *Samuel Beckett: A Collection of Critical Essays*, Prentice-Hall, Englewood Cliffs, New Jersey, 1965.

Dougald McMillan and Martha Fehsenfeld, *Beckett in the Theatre: The Author as Practical Playwright and Director*, Volume I: *From 'Waiting for Godot' to 'Krapp's Last Tape'*, John Calder, London and Riverrun Press, New York, 1988.

John Fletcher, *Samuel Beckett's Art*, Chatto & Windus, London, 1967.

Alan Warren Friedman, Charles Rossman, and Dina Sherzer, *Beckett Translating/Translating Beckett*, The Pennsylvania State University Press, University Park and London, 1987.

S.E. Gontarski, editor, *On Beckett: Essays and Criticism*, Grove Press, New York, 1986.

Lawrence Graver and Raymond Federman, *Samuel Beckett: The Critical Heritage*, Routledge & Kegan aul, London, 1979.

Lawrence Harvey, *Samuel Beckett Poet and Critic, Princeton University Press, Princeton, New Jersey, 1970.*

Hugh Kenner, A Reader's Guide to Samuel Beckett, Thames & Hudson, London, 1973.

James Knowlson, 'Beckett as Director: The Manuscript Production Notebooks and Critical Interpretation', *Modern Drama*, XXX, 4 December 1987, pp. 451–65.

James Knowlson and John Pilling, *Frescoes of the Skull: The Later Prose and Drama of Samuel Beckett*, John Calder, London, 1979.

Charles R. Lyons, *Samuel Beckett*, Macmillan, London, 1983.

Vivian Mercier, *Beckett/Beckett*, Oxford University Press, 1977.

Edouard Morot-Sir, et al., *Samuel Beckett: The Art of Rhetoric*, North Carolina Studies in Romance Languages and Literature, Chapel Hill, 1976.

Kristin Morrison, *Canters and Chronicles: The Use of Narrative in the Plays of Samuel Beckett and Harold Pinter*, University of Chicago Press, Chicago and London, 1983.

Michael Robinson, *The Long Sonata of the Dead: A Study of Samuel Beckett*, Hart-Davis, London, 1969.

Alan Schneider, *Entrances*, New York, Viking, 1986.

Thomas R. Whitaker, ' "Wham, Bam, Thank you Sam": The Presence of Beckett', in Brater, *Beckett at 80/ Beckett in Context, see above*.

Katherine Worth, editor, *Beckett the Shape Changer*, Routledge & Kegan Paul, London and Boston, 1975.

Studies and criticism of *Waiting for Godot*

Walter Asmus, 'Beckett Directs *Godot*', *Theatre Quarterly*, 5 (September, November 1975), pp. 19–26.

Peter Bull, *I Know the Face, But*, Peter Davies, London 1959.

Frederick Busi, *The Transformations of Godot*, The University Press of Kentucky, Lexington, Kentucky, 1980.

Ruby Cohn, editor, *Casebook on Waiting for Godot*, Grove Press, New York, 1967.

Colin Duckworth, '*Beckett's New Godot*', in *Beckett's Later Fiction and Drama*, edited by James Acheson and Kateryna Arthur, St Martin's Press, New York, 1987, pp. 175–92.

editor, *En attendant Godot*, Harrap, London, 1966.

Beryl S. and John Fletcher, *A Student's Guide to the Plays of Samuel Beckett*, second edition, Faber & Faber, London, 1985, pp. 42–76.

Harold Hobson, 'Samuel Beckett, Dramatist of the Year', in *International Theatre Annual*, No. 1, John Calder, London, 1956, pp. 153–5.

Bernard Lalande, '*En attendant Godot*', Hatier, Coll. Profit d'une œuvre, Paris, 1970.

Emile Lavielle, '*En attendant Godot*' de Beckett, Hachette, Coll. Poche Critique, Paris, 1972.

J.P. Little, '*En attendant Godot*' and '*Fin de Partie*': Critical Guides to French Texts, Grant & Cutler Ltd., London, 1981.

Anne C. Murch, 'Quoting from *Godot*: Trends in Contemporary French Theatre', *Journal of Beckett Studies*, No. 9, 1984, pp. 113–29.

Bert O. States, *The Shape of Paradox: An Essay on 'Waiting for Godot'*, University of California Press, Berkeley and Los Angeles, 1978.

Clas Zilliacus, 'Three Times *Godot*: Beckett, Brecht, Bulatović', *Comparative Drama*, IV, 1 (Spring 1970), pp. 3–17.

Studies of modern drama and related works

Susan Brienza, 'Sam No. 2: Shepard Plays Beckett with an American Accent', in *Beckett Translating/Translating Beckett*, The Pennsylvania State University Press, University Park and London, 1987.

Peter Brook, *The Shifting Point: Theatre, Film, Opera 1946–1987*, Harper and Row, New York, 1987.

John Calder, *As No Other Dare Fail*, John Calder, London, 1986.

Martin Esslin, *The Theatre of the Absurd*, third edition, Penguin Books, Harmondsworth, 1980.

Roger Fowler, *Modern Critical Terms*, London and New York, Routledge & Kegan Paul, 1987.

Athol Fugard, *Notebooks: 1960–1977*, Alfred Knopf, New York, 1984.

John Goodwin, editor, *Peter Hall's Diaries*, London, 1983.

Ronald Hayman, *Tom Stoppard*, Rowman, London, 1979.

James Lord, *Giacometti*, Farrar, Straus and Giroux, New York, 1985.

John Peter, *Vladimir's Carrot: Modern Drama and the Modern Imagination*, Andre Deutsch, London, 1987.

Jordan R. Young, *The Beckett Actor: Jack MacGowran, Beginning to End*, Moonstone Press, Beverly Hills, California, 1987.